Dedication

In Search of Revival is dedicated to Geoffrey Bell, my dad, who went to be with the Lord while this book was being written. His desire for "more" of God and his ability to adapt and change with the passing of time have encouraged me to enter into everything that God has planned for me.

Acknowledgments

My thanks and appreciation go to the following people:

Irene, my wife and best friend.

Andrew, Becki, and David, my children.

Betty, my mum.

Val Seager, for her checking of manuscripts, regular communication with the U.S.A., and personal support and encouragement.

Gerald Coates, for his wise counsel and loving concern through the years, and for his helpful input.

Jack and Tricia Groblewski, our closest friends.

Simon Fox, who originally encouraged me to write.

The leaders and members of New Life Christian Fellowship, Lincoln.

Members of the Ground Level Team.

The Destiny Image family, for drawing a book out of me.

Contents

Endorsements   vi

Foreword   vii

Introduction   ix

Chapter 1   Hunger and Thirst Ignites the Fire   1

Chapter 2   The Loud-Voiced Church   11

Chapter 3   Hope in the Hand of God   29

Chapter 4   Hear the Lion's Roar!   49

Chapter 5   Awakening the Oil-Filled Church   67

Chapter 6   Rediscover the Power of Blessing   81

Chapter 7   Discern the Pressures of Progress and
Hindrances to Revival   97

Chapter 8   Building a Team   117

Chapter 9   Pursue God's Vision   141

Chapter 10 Become a Church of Influence   161

Endorsements

The Church worldwide is seeing the beginnings of revival in our generation and Stuart Bell is emerging as one of its humble yet powerful leaders. *In Search of Revival* captures God's heartbeat for reviving both a dry spirit and a dry church. It answers the "What's next?" question. Containing so much meat you will want to refer to it again and again, this book has the potential to become a revival classic.
—*Melinda Fish*, Author and International Speaker

Far too much thinking, praying, and reading of revival has romanticized the situations we find ourselves in. Stuart Bell does not fall into this trap. Whereas he inspires us in the search for revival, he also challenges us to align our lives, our methodologies, and our ministry functions with the purpose of God for our time. Revival is not simply a matter of God's doing it all, but rather God's doing it in response to the faith and obedience of a people in search of revival.
—*Bryn Jones*, Founder of Covenant Ministries Intl.

My very first encounter with Stuart Bell proved to be my "undoing." I and some other pastors in our city were catapulted into an arena of prayer from which we've dared not retreat. He too is a "carrier" of the purpose of God; it is my prayer that you will be infected and affected by this heavenly "virus" of unabashed love for the Father. If I had any confusion about revival, it all became clear. I found myself saying, as I read this wonderful book, "It's about prayer, stupid!"
—*Joseph L. Garlington*, Pastor of Covenant Church of Pittsburgh

Stuart Bell achieves an uncommon blend—a serious book for popular use, a popular book for serious reading. With wisdom and common sense, he engages the topic of revival to provide a clear understanding of its meaning (the what) and method (the how). I warmly commend Stuart Bell's book, a richly balanced, profoundly original explanation of the meaning and fundamental structure of active revival.
—*Jay Johns*, Philo Trust

Rooted in the lessons from Scripture, but full of modern day stories, Stuart Bell describes his search for revival.
—*Gerald Coates*, Speaker, Author, Broadcaster

Foreword

I regard it as a privilege to write a Foreword for my friend Stuart Bell. The book he has written addresses the current movement of the Holy Spirit that has crossed nearly every denominational line as well as geographical boundary.

Stuart Bell is pastor of one of the liveliest, most influential churches in England. I have preached there a number of times, and I know of the way God has used his church generally and Stuart Bell himself particularly. (Stuart is pastor to the well-known songwriter and musician Chris Bowater.)

I must admit that I blushed as I read Stuart's references to me in the early part of the book. I am not worthy of such accolades and can only say that I am surprised that God used me as He apparently did. When I prayed for Stuart, I can state categorically that I did not feel a thing and was not the slightest bit conscious of being any "carrier" of God's blessing.

I believe that we are in the embryonic phase of the greatest work of the Holy Spirit in this century—and it wouldn't surprise me if it turns out to be the greatest movement since the early Church. It is what I've looked forward to all my life, and it is only the beginning. In fact, what we've experienced up to now is what Paul Cain calls the "appetizer," and the main course is at hand.

Stuart describes how deeply people have been blessed by what we might call the "starters" of God's blessing. The stories will convince any open-minded skeptic that what has been going on for the past three years or more is truly from the God of the Bible. I myself, when I first heard about this move, said that it was not of God. I had to climb down after a closer examination, and it wasn't an easy thing for me to have to do. But I've known for years how God uses the foolish things of this world to confound the wise (see 1 Cor. 1:27), and this refers not only to the way He saves people and the kind of people whom He saves, but also to God's general dealings. You could call it His sense of humor! It puts the sophisticated off, and just as the common people heard Jesus gladly, so this movement is an appeal to those who are largely rejected by the Church generally. There are exceptions, of course, but this is a movement of the Spirit for those who are willing to go "outside the camp" (Heb. 13:13).

Stuart does not claim to have all the answers to the questions one might ask, and the best of people will want to debate some of the ways he interprets things. But he believes that we must be ready for what God is going to do in our churches, and the book touches on pertinent, practical issues.

I pray that this book will have a wide circulation and be a blessing to all who read these lines—and most of all that it will bring great honor and glory to God.

R.T. Kendall
Westminster Chapel
London

Introduction

From an early age I had a strange fascination for revival. As a boy I heard stories about the early growth of Methodism and was impressed with the ministry of John Wesley. My dad was a local preacher for over 25 years and I remember him taking me to many of his preaching appointments. I couldn't help noticing, however, that the "chapels" we visited didn't seem to be surging with new life or new growth. In fact, the congregations were usually composed of elderly people. I was impressed with their sincerity, but I was looking for a greater expression of fervent faith in God.

A search for revival had begun, and from time to time a group of us teenagers in our church would spend time asking God to send revival. I also began to reason that not only was God's *favor* important in preparation for Him to move, but also people's *fervor*. I had been told that "prayer always precedes power."

Together with my personal desires for more of God, I began to sense God's call on my life with regard to the importance of Church. I wasn't looking for something that would just be a personal blessing; I was looking for communities of God's people to be energized by God's power and then released to affect the world around them. It seems to me that the "Great Commandment" and the "Great Commission" are two vital ingredients in this. If a group of people who love one another and who love God could be empowered to "go into all the world and preach the good news," what could happen? Church history reveals many occasions when God's presence and power impacted people to such an extent that the very social fabric of society was affected.

I am aware that the word *revival* is on many lips at this time, and those people who have a theological disposition to do so, will debate whether we are looking for renewal, refreshing, restoration, revival, or awakening. I have chosen to use the word *revival* in a general sense, one that encompasses the above. I like the definition used by Duncan Campbell, who was involved in the Hebridean revival of 1949. He described revival as "a community saturated with God" (*Compass Magazine*, Winter 1997/98—a Pioneer/Ground Level publication). I am looking for signs of God impacting individuals, families, and churches so that the good news of Jesus can be shared in word, life, and action to a world that desperately needs it.

In my late teens I was deeply impacted through the baptism of the Holy Spirit. This experience changed the course of my life and became the foundation for every encounter with God that followed.

In May 1994 I was surprised by a season of refreshing from the Lord that reawakened a desire in me to move forward in my search for revival. Within a few weeks, Irene, my wife, was testifying to having a new confidence in serving God. This has been confirmed regularly by her vocal contributions in meetings and by a new boldness in speaking out. Andrew, my 24-year-old son, has exhibited every kind of outward sign of God's touch, from laughter to shaking, and has changed almost beyond recognition. He is now in youth leadership. Becki, my daughter, aged 21, was also impacted deeply, and over the last two years has been actively involved in Christian work within dance, TV, and frontline evangelism. David, my youngest, aged 11, has requested prayer at every opportunity and we have seen him develop a very sensitive and compassionate heart toward people who are sick or hurting.

When God visits our families and then brings new life to the wider body of the Church within a short period of time, it reignites our desires for God to come. What God has given to us needs to be given away and shared.

This book was written with a deep desire to share, within the framework of Scripture, some of the wonderful things that God is doing today. It is for everyone who wants "more."

Chapter 1

Hunger and Thirst Ignites the Fire

My search for God's Presence had been going strong since I was eight years old, but I never thought I would encounter God's fire *this* way. After all, I was standing before the eminent Doctor R.T. Kendall, the minister of London's Westminster Chapel, and one of England's most respected Christian scholars and churchmen. He occupied a high office held by a succession of famous scholars and clergymen, including most recently the late D. Martyn Lloyd-Jones, the celebrated author of the classic work, *Surprised By Joy*.

Dr. R.T. Kendall was definitely not known as a Charismatic, but he had agreed to speak to our non-denominational church on the topic, "The Spirit and the Word." He had originally taken a stand against the "Toronto Blessing," but admitted, "I hoped I was wrong." Because he's a very humble man, Dr. Kendall asked questions to find out more about this apparent move of God. Finally he asked to talk with members of London's Holy Trinity Brompton Anglican Church, who had been personally impacted by the renewal.

We, too, had heard rumors of the move of God in Canada and then in London, and by the time Dr. Kendall had reached my church, New Life Christian Fellowship in Lincoln, he had come to believe that the renewal was a genuine move of God. True to form, he told his church that he'd changed his opinions but was concerned that he never seemed to experience any of the outward signs of the renewal.

We were sharing a meal together after the meeting, and this man, who had preached on revival for years, began to ask some very penetrating questions. Dr. Kendall was widely respected for his strength of character, solid conservatism, and brilliant intellect, yet his comments about revival were very, very interesting. He said, "I have prayed for revival all my life, but I wonder if I will recognize it when it comes? Will I be able to cope with the packaging in which God sends it?" I think this is often the case for many church leaders around the world.

Dr. Kendall began to talk about the renewal that was sweeping through some of London's most significant churches, and how Westminster Chapel had seemingly been bypassed. Then he said, "You know, I've not been touched by this—I never felt anything." I could tell he was genuinely bothered by that fact, and I remember saying to him, "We shouldn't rely on our feelings...perhaps you are a *carrier* of this blessing, you see."

At first I thought I had offended the man. Dr. Kendall suddenly became very quiet, and as my alarm grew, he looked at me and said, "Have you ever used that word before?" I thought, *Now I'm in for it.* So I said, "No, it just came into my head." (Again, that is not a thing to say to a great leader.)

R.T. Kendall was very strong on Calvinism. So I assumed, rightly or wrongly, that he was struggling with the concept of being a carrier of God's blessing, and that I had unknowingly used a word that was quite important to him theologically.

So there we were one fine evening in May of 1994. My casual comment had apparently caused one of England's great churchmen to grow suddenly silent and remain so for some time. Meanwhile, I was mentally wondering what apology would do. To my surprise Dr. Kendall asked later that evening, *"I need to know whether I'm a carrier.* Can I pray with you before I leave?"

As he stood in my church office with me and two of my ministry team members, we were keenly aware that this man wasn't just some enthusiastic Pentecostal talking about renewal this way—this was *Dr. Kendall.*

Now Dr. R.T. Kendall did not come from a background where he laid hands on people or anything like that which smacked of Pentecostalism, so he just stood there in the room—almost awkwardly—and prayed, "Lord, if in any way I've been a carrier of this blessing, touch my friends. Bless them and anoint them with Your Spirit." And that was it. No trembling lips, shaking knees, ecstatic words, or even a hint of passion. It was quite amazing because my brain was telling me one thing, and my heart was saying something else. My brain was saying, "This man doesn't believe in this." Yet my heart was saying, "God is in this place."

After the prayer, Dr. Kendall told us, "If anything happens in the next 24 hours, write to me first class!" None of us particularly "felt" anything, but we promised this great conservative church leader that we would honor his request. On the drive home that night, although I had experienced no extraordinary feelings or sensations, I still sensed that God had nonetheless done something.

The following morning, I drove to the East Coast of England to teach some sessions at a retreat for the Ichthus association of churches at Sizewell Hall. I felt a growing sense of excitement that morning as I reflected on the events of the previous night with Dr. Kendall, and on the fact that some of the Ichthus churches had already been impacted by the move of the Spirit.

I began to teach at 10:30 that morning, and it quickly became evident that the Presence of God was very tangible in the place. At one point in the meeting, I was praying with Roger Forster, another respected national leader, when suddenly the power of God broke out in the meeting. People began to do some unusual things that I really hadn't seen before! I was amazed to see people begin to shake and laugh uncontrollably, though I was a bit more comfortable when I saw people start to frankly confess their sins to one another. (Now *that* was something I could recognize as "acceptable.") In the end, my level of surprise or discomfort didn't seem to matter because that intense level of spiritual visitation and ministry continued unbroken for a full five hours!

I was so moved emotionally by God's sudden descent on His people that I just wanted to go home and think it over. But God wasn't about to allow me the luxury of contemplation. I was already committed to speak at yet another meeting that evening with the leaders of Newark Baptist Church, which was situated along my route home about 16 miles (20 km) from Lincoln. A friend named Bill Prentice had come along with me for this one-day ministry trip, and we talked the entire length of the drive to Newark.

The meeting was a low-key affair being held at someone's home. Everything seemed to go smoothly until the pastor of the church asked us to pray with the small group of leaders before we left. As soon as we prayed, those phenomena began to appear again among these Baptist leaders! This time Bill and I were caught up in the move of the Spirit too!

I began to laugh uncontrollably, and so did Bill. This was remarkable in his case since Bill was still recovering from injuries suffered in a major automobile accident, and he was naturally avoiding the painful effects of laughter whenever possible. He didn't even try to resist that night—we were firmly in the gentle grips of supernatural laughter triggered by a refreshing from the Lord.

Now Bill and I had left home at 6:00 that morning to get to Sizewell, so when the clock struck 11:00 that night, I told the pastor of that Baptist church that we would have to begin our journey home. Since at that moment he was still lying helplessly on the floor under the power of God, he managed to say, "Just let yourselves out, if you don't mind. I don't think I can manage it just now."

I didn't have much time to reflect on the oddity of our parting scene at the Newark Baptist Church meeting because Bill and I faced our own crisis on the way to the car. Yes, I have a background in the Pentecostal and Charismatic movement, but I have never been known as an emotional thrill-seeker or an excitable religious type. I suppose I am considered a conservative by many who know me. I was glad they couldn't see me that night in Newark.

Bill and I faced a difficult struggle just to walk to the car! Anyone watching us that night would have written us off because we were staggering like two drunks who had lingered too long over their beers. I had problems even remembering how to get the key into the ignition, so you can imagine what we faced during the drive home that night! (What made it especially difficult was the fact that, for the life of me, I just couldn't stop laughing.)

By God's grace we finally managed to make our way safely home. Bill told me later that when he crawled into bed that night, his wife awoke, and as he told her about what had happened to us, she, too, erupted into uncontrollable laughter! Somehow the blessing Bill had experienced in Newark had been passed on to his wife merely because she was near him!

When morning dawned, I knew that a new day had come to my life. For some reason I also sensed that my church would never be the same either. When I began to share my experiences with my family and church members, the same kind of phenomena started to affect them too. The new "blessing" from God began to break into the life of the local church almost overnight.

That same day, I wrote a letter to Dr. Kendall outlining what had happened and sent it first class. I quickly received R.T.'s brief reply:

"Dear Stuart, wow, w-o-w."

Since that time in the summer of 1994, Dr. Kendall has received his own personal confirmation of God's blessing on his life. When he was invited to speak at Toronto Airport Christian Fellowship, I decided to go to support him. While Dr. Kendall was speaking, the anointing of God overcame him so powerfully that he seemed to be drunk in the Spirit! I can still hear him saying over and over in slurred speech, "This is going to get back to England...this is on video," and he was quite embarrassed because he couldn't get through his material! He said, "Please pray for me, I can't..." and would trail off until another partial phrase would come. It is a videotape that is "worth the price of admission" because it's so funny.

Dr. Kendall has paid a high price in this renewal in terms of losing a number of members in his church because of his willingness to identify with Toronto Airport Christian Fellowship and with Rodney Howard-Browne.

Now with such a grand preface, I can better explain my purpose for writing this book. Return to the haunting words R.T. Kendall spoke over the dinner table that summer night in 1994: "I have prayed for revival all my life, but I wonder if I will recognize it when it comes? Will I be able to cope with the packaging in which God sends it?"

My heart burns for every precious person who risks the danger of overlooking God's visitation because he or she doesn't recognize the "wrapping paper" or delivery company. What if the blind man, Bartimaeus, had failed to cry out to Jesus when He passed by? Even worse, what if he had listened to the negative voices of men and remained silent?

I'll tell you what would have happened: Bartimaeus would have spent the rest of his days begging by the roadside in Jericho. He would have died in his spiritual and physical poverty and he would have died without sight—having never looked into the wonderful face of Jesus. Furthermore, his children would have been doomed to follow in his spiritually downtrodden footsteps.

Bartimaeus is a Chaldean name that literally means "son (*bar*) of contamination or foulness (*tame*)"[1], so this poor man grew up hearing his own father being called "foulness or contamination" every single day. The Cure for our miserable condition in the Church and in the world is only a heart cry away, yet millions are refusing to call out, or are afraid to seek God's touch in this great revival because of the negative shouting of men!

I had been searching for more of God for decades before the Lord so graciously touched me that night in 1994. I had already experienced the genuine thrill of salvation when I came to Christ as a boy, and later I received the baptism of the Holy Spirit, a life-changing encounter that has remained central to my faith. But all along I somehow knew there was *more*, and I made it my personal quest to find it. There are multiplied millions of Christians who long for more of God like me, and even more people who simply want to meet God for the first time but don't know how. They desperately need to hear the truth about God. They need some help on their search for God and their quest for fire.

God has begun to move among people of many nations on a level that seems ready to outstrip every previous outpouring, renewal, awakening, or reformation in human history! He is sweeping thousands into the Kingdom every week in North and South America, Europe, Asia, and the many island nations of the earth. Millions are discovering dimensions of the spirit that they never dreamed existed. And while the secular media around the world is greeting this spiritual upheaval with at least an open-minded interest, many in the so-called religious press have set their hearts and their mouths against it.

In response, I believe God is raising up what I call a "loud-voiced Church." I consider myself to be just one of millions of "loud-mouths" anointed by God to raise my voice on behalf of the poor, the hurting, and the hungry people around me. They don't need to hear the negative voices of critics; they need to call out to Jesus Christ in the midst of the crowd. They need to cry out until they hear His voice for themselves and personally feel the healing touch of His Presence and power. Jesus is visiting this planet in an especially tangible way in this worldwide revival, and it is time for us to cry out His name.

Weary church pastors in virtually every nation around the world need to receive answers to their honest questions about this move of God. It is for people who are on a search that I write this book. They are on a holy quest, a divine mission commissioned by God Himself. Some seek the Kingdom;

some seek comfort. Some seek the inheritance they never knew they had, and others seek the righteousness they never knew they could have. Others seek mercy in a world (and Church) too quick to judge, but almost all of them hope to see God somehow. These people qualify for the promise Jesus gave them 2,000 years ago:

Blessed are the poor in spirit, for theirs is the kingdom of heaven. Blessed are those who mourn, for they will be comforted. Blessed are the meek, for they will inherit the earth. Blessed are those who hunger and thirst for righteousness, for they will be filled. Blessed are the merciful, for they will be shown mercy. Blessed are the pure in heart, for they will see God (Matthew 5:3-8).

I have good news. My search for fire led me right into a divine appointment with God, an encounter He had planned long ago. I earnestly believe that the seekers who pick up this book were launched on their journey by the very One whom they seek. I believe He has ordained a meeting in the near future that will change their lives forever. Again I return to the sure words of Jesus, who promised you and I:

Ask and it will be given to you; seek and you will find; knock and the door will be opened to you. For everyone who asks receives; he who seeks finds; and to him who knocks, the door will be opened. Which of you, if his son asks for bread, will give him a stone? Or if he asks for a fish, will give him a snake? If you, then, though you are evil, know how to give good gifts to your children, how much more will your Father in heaven give good gifts to those who ask Him! (Matthew 7:7-11)

God loves to meet people on a search. Over and over again, He has declared His delight with what many call "seekers." He said through the voice of wisdom, "I love those who love Me, and those who seek Me find Me" (Prov. 8:17); and "You will seek Me and find Me when you seek Me with all your heart" (Jer. 29:13). In the Book of Hosea, the prophet of God declares something to captive Israel that many Christians today don't want to hear, let alone apply to the chastised Church of our day:

> *Come, let us return to the Lord. He has torn us to pieces but He will heal us; He has injured us but He will bind up our wounds. After two days He will revive us; on the third day He will restore us, that we may live in His presence* (Hosea 6:1-2).

Nearly every leader in the Church worldwide will agree that we have endured more than a decade of spiritual dryness, a long drought during which many believers have longed for a refreshing and a fresh visitation from on High. More than anything else, the chief fruit of the 1980's and 90's has been a healthy hunger and thirst for more of God and less of the flesh. God has heard our cries and launched us by the millions on a holy quest for the fire of His Presence and glory, and the goal of our search is simply God and nothing else. The first sign and proof that God has visited our land is the appearance of the loud-voiced Church.

Endnote

1. James Strong, *Strong's Exhaustive Concordance of the Bible* (Peabody, MA: Hendrickson Publishers, n.d.) **Bartimaeus** (Greek, #924) and (Hebrew, #2931).

Chapter 2

The Loud-Voiced Church

For nearly a decade in the 1930's, high winds and merciless drought took advantage of years of improper farming practices to hold the normally fertile Midwest region of the United States hostage. Millions of tons of rich topsoil disappeared in vast billowing black clouds, only to be replaced by layer upon layer of infertile mounds of sand.

On the very heels of America's "Great Depression," the country's formerly stable farming economy was suddenly—and literally—blown to the winds. The old ways just wouldn't do anymore because the depleted soil wouldn't produce crops. Hundreds of thousands of newly homeless farmers were forced to migrate westward along "Route 66," the infamous "Dustbowl Highway" to California in hopes of a fresh start. Drought brought dramatic change to every aspect of life for these refugees of circumstance who came to be called "Okies."

In our day, the Church worldwide has endured its own decade of drought, and again hunger and thirst have brought change. In this case, it is a welcome change for good. In the years before the dry times, we were content to tend to our own best interests with little concern for the welfare of others or for preaching the gospel to the lost.

Now, after enduring long years of spiritual apathy, hunger, thirst, division, and barrenness, God's people have suddenly gotten so desperate for God that they have dropped their flags of division and symbols of schism. Their hunger has so overpowered their fear of one another that they have begun to cry out to God side by side with one voice and one accord—exactly as God always intended.

The Scriptures show us that from time to time, the people of God have raised their voices and become a "loud-voiced people" who cried out to God in fervent prayer and intercession. Perhaps like me, you will admit that there has been a big gap in your life between what you knew you were to be doing and what you actually did in your prayer life (personally and corporately in the church).

If you have been a Christian for ten years or more, you may have some amusing (or embarrassing) memories of past prayer meetings marked by a distinct lack of power and chronically poor attendance. In this new day of God's visitation, we desperately need to learn how to pray *together* and hungrily seek the face of the Lord in one accord. It is the "loud-voiced church" that experiences the outpouring of the Holy Spirit and true revival!

At times I have prayed like the disciples in the Gospels, "Lord, teach us how to pray." My memories of prayer meetings used to bring up images of laborious meetings with the same "faithful handful" of people each week, many of whom seemed determined to pray exceptionally long prayers fitted with many words and little power. Yes, there has always been a remnant of people in every generation who managed to press in to God in prayer and intercession, but this anointing has rarely made it into the life of the Church as a whole.

However, whenever the Church has moved forward in the purposes of God, it very often began to rise up in prayer *first*. In times of genuine revival, the Church often becomes the loud-voiced Church. I began to search the Scriptures for this pattern because the British Church in particular often thinks of prayer as something rather quiet and personal. We tend to think more of having our own quiet times than of fervent corporate prayer meetings. I discovered that there was a strong theological position for both the Church praying *together* as well as our usual *private prayer stance*.

Obviously we are to pray in our prayer rooms and seek Him as individuals, but we have no grounds for discarding fervent corporate prayer. I discovered precious few models in our generation that conform to the kind of prayer we often see in Scripture, and most of those arose as part of this great move of God on the Church in our day.

Loud-Voiced Prayers in the Bible

When King Asa brought reforms to the people of God, the Bible says, "They took an oath to the Lord with *loud acclamation, with shouting and with trumpets and with horns*" (2 Chron. 15:14). When Asa confronted the binding effects of compromise and idolatry in the life of the people, they shouted to God in joyful response. This is a picture of God's loud-voiced people expressing their hunger for His glory, His favor, and His Word.

When King Jehoshaphat made bold advances in the purposes of God in Second Chronicles 20:19, the Bible says that they "stood up and praised the Lord, the God of Israel, with *very loud voice.*"

I am intrigued by this passage. Every time the people of God begin to advance toward Him in the Bible, they become a loud-voiced people. In the Books of Ezra and Nehemiah, when the temple of the Lord was being rebuilt and the broken walls of Jerusalem were being restored, God's people responded with loud voices. Ezra declared, "The whole assembly responded with a *loud voice*" (Ezra 10:12a). Nehemiah said that they "called with *loud voices* to the Lord their God" (Neh. 9:4).

Some people object, saying, "Well, you should know that concerns the ancient Jewish culture—not our modern civilized culture." (I can barely resist asking folks who ask me if this in my country: "Don't you watch television? What do we 'self-controlled Brits' do during the national soccer championships?")

The "loud voices" described in these Old Testament passages probably refer more to the amplified effect of everyone raising their voices together than to the extreme volume of just a few raised voices. Throughout the Old Testament we see the people of God begin to advance when He plants a cause in their hearts and raises their levels of expectation. Invariably a corporate loudness begins to rise from their assembly to the Lord.

This pattern shows up again among members of the early Church in two passages found in the Book of Acts. The first is found in Acts 4:24, after the Jewish Sanhedrin (supreme court) had forbidden the apostles to use the name of Jesus publicly: "When they [the believers] heard this, *they raised their voices together* in prayer to God..." Then again in Acts 12, we find Peter locked away in Herod's prison facing an almost certain appointment with death: "So Peter was kept in prison, but *the church was earnestly praying* to God for him" (Acts 12:5). The Greek word translated as "earnestly praying" means "fervent, stretched, zealous, or earnest." If the entire Church in Jerusalem was praying fervently, zealously, and earnestly—and stretching themselves in the effort—it is difficult to imagine them praying silently or even quietly. No, this is a picture of a red-hot *loud-voiced* prayer meeting.

When the people of God become a loud-voiced people determined to touch the heart of God, their strength isn't necessarily found in the volume of individual voices. It is found in their joined voices raised to God *corporately* as one voice.

Loud-Voiced Prayer Always Precedes Revival

Every outpouring of the Holy Spirit and season of revival have been preceded and accompanied by prayer. I believe God is calling all of us to prayer in these days of worldwide renewal and revival. A number of Brazilian pastors were instructed by God to move from Brazil to Great Britain, and some of them gave up very large churches to obey God's call to stand alongside British churches. Why did they make such a sacrifice? They were convinced that revival was on the way. By mid-1997, those Brazilian pastors had built a network of well over 100 English churches who were committed to 40 days of prayer and fasting before the Lord. This isn't the time to say, "Well, what's everybody else doing? Let's jump on the bandwagon." However, there is a grass roots sense that God is doing something significant in the world, and I believe our Father is looking for a loud-voiced Church to emerge.

I was invited to speak at a "refreshing meeting" during the 1997 Spring Harvest, an annual Christian gathering that draws 80,000 people every year. Although it is not a Charismatic event, more and more people have begun to attend special meetings devoted to renewal or revival. I was supposed to do just one of these "refreshing" meetings, and I ended up being involved in one every night of the conference! Five years ago, if you had conducted a seminar on the

Holy Spirit, you might have drawn 60 people. The times have changed. By the second night of the conference, the leaders were talking about having to close the "refreshing" venue because between 600 and 800 people were turning up late at night to receive prayer and the empowering of the Holy Spirit!

I can't stress enough how important it is for us to continually seek the Lord and wait upon Him in this hour. Most of us will agree intellectually with this statement, thinking, *If we are asking God to move, we need to pray.* Now we need to go beyond thought to action. We need to "make the connection" in prayer. Many of us have been praying all our lives, but we still feel like we've hardly started. There is a lot we can discover about corporate prayer in the Church. Perhaps we need to look at other cultures to learn how to pray. This much is sure: If we want to see God move in power, then we need to make connections in prayer as a loud-voiced Church.

What Causes or Creates a Loud-Voiced Church?

Are there any ingredients that brought the people of God to raise their voices together to Him? I have found at least four common ingredients in God's Word.

1. *When the Church is under pressure,* God's people are transformed into a loud-voiced Church. Ezra and Nehemiah each faced great opposition when they rallied the Israelites to rebuild the temple in Jerusalem. There was also strong opposition to the rebuilding of the wall surrounding Old Jerusalem. These leaders endured extreme pressure when they boldly challenged the compromise that had enslaved God's people. The people of God were under pressure.

Pressure is not always bad—especially when it comes from or is permitted by the Lord. Regardless of the source, I believe that when a church is under pressure, it begins to raise its voice to the Lord. The apostles were under pressure in Acts 4 after the Jewish leaders ordered them to stop speaking in the name of Jesus. The first thing the local church did was to call a prayer meeting! Then they raised their voices together in unified, fervent prayer. Why? They were under pressure.

"Well, the apostles were different from us, don't you see? They could cope with pressure better than we can. They were a different breed of men who were braver and bolder than we are." That's simply not true, but if you insist on believing that lie, then what are you going to do with the general believers who had to survive while watching their key leaders put to death one after another? Surely they were at least a little like us today! The early believers in the Jerusalem Church in Acts 12 experienced *extreme pressure* after their pastor, James, was beheaded by Herod's men. Things got even worse when Herod had Peter the apostle thrown in jail, too, with obvious intentions to execute him as well. Every human instinct in the surviving apostles and church members said, "Let's back off; perhaps we shouldn't go for this." But they called a prayer meeting and passionately raised their voices to God. Why? The church was under pressure.

The Church experiences extreme pressure in many parts of the world today, yet revival is beginning to sweep through those areas as never before! Thousands are facing death and persecution every day in Vietnam, China, India, Pakistan, and many other places as satan arouses the hatred of governments and violent religious movements against Christians. Because the people of God have responded with raised voices in unified prayer, revival has sprung up out of the pressure, persecution, and pain. True revival springs from true prayer. The pressured Church becomes a loud-voiced Church whose voice is always heard by the living God. The Church around the world faces pressure on every front as governments, societies, and human moral standards continue to quickly move further and further away from the truth of God's Word.

2. *When the Church gets desperate*, God's people are transformed into a loud-voiced Church. In Ezra 10:1-2 and Nehemiah 10:39, the people of God became desperate when they recognized their dire need and realized how low they had fallen. Once their eyes were opened to their dangerous condition, they began to cry out to the Lord in repentance and vow, "We will not neglect the house of our God" (Neh. 10:39b).

I often find that after I complete an extended period of prayer and fasting, the Lord hasn't necessarily given me great release or spiritual empowerment. Rather, He has opened my eyes to my own condition in areas where I have not relied solely upon Him. I emerge from my time of consecration with a new sense of my own unworthiness and weakness, and I am more keenly aware than ever of my complete inability to do what God is calling me to! Is this discouraging? No, it is my salvation. It is a wake-up call, an alarm that faithfully directs my gaze back to my Savior, my sole source of love, wisdom, and power. I believe with all my heart that we've got to get desperate before the Lord.

We all have some very important choices to make each day. Yes, we can choose to be people who go through life with a mediocre approach to things—especially where the Church is concerned. I am very aware that not everyone reading this book is actively looking for the things that I'm looking for. You may not be looking for a great move of God in the Holy Spirit, but I tell you I am looking for nothing less than a complete revival of the supernatural Church of Jesus Christ in our day. The mediocre approach won't do in the revived Church of fire. I don't say this to be condemning, but God Himself is challenging our priorities and daily choices in life.

What comes first in your life? I was asked to talk about *idolatry* at the Spring Harvest meetings. Now I'd never spoken on that subject before, but the reality is that many of us—yes, I'm talking about Christian people—have idols. We may not have a stone image of baal on the mantel at home, but we have placed things ahead of or before the living and eternal God.

The more I go on in the ministry, the more I see things being set before me. I'm beginning to get desperate. In our local situation, I know that our city desperately needs to hear the gospel proclaimed—and it is up to the people of God to get the job done. We need to recognize that we must have breakthroughs to proclaim the Word of God with power and authority. We need to get desperate. We need to live in the reality that the Church is meant to move in supernatural faith and power as a visible demonstration of the life and love of God. We need to ask ourselves some serious questions:

- Are we truly Pentecostal people?
- Are we truly Charismatic people?
- Do we really believe in the God of miracles?
- Do we actually believe that God still heals today?

Most Christians have seen very little evidence of God's power in their lives, but the Word of God declares that God is the same yesterday, today, and forever (see Heb. 13:8). Jesus is still the eternal Son of God, and though we have not seen the spectacular in our own experience as in the days of the acts of the apostles, I put it to you that we need to be rising in faith! We need to get desperate and cry out to God with a loud voice in unity. We need to dare to believe the gospel to be the power of God unto salvation (see Rom. 1:16).

3. *When the Church pleads Scripture,* God's people are transformed into a loud-voiced Church. I find it interesting that in every Bible passage we've examined in this chapter, the people of God raised their voices together and expressed their reverence and worship to the sovereign Lord, the God who always faithfully keeps His promises to man. In Nehemiah 9, the Israelites began to proclaim the sovereign power of God and recounted His faithfulness. As they entered into prayer, they reminded one another of their history with the God who delivered them from Egypt and led them to Canaan. They reminded one another of the roots of their faith, and they began to proclaim Scripture.

The same thing happened in Acts 4:24-30, when the Jewish believers raised their voices together to proclaim the sovereignty of God by reciting the second Psalm. What were they doing? They were humbly bringing Scripture back to the Lord—they were pleading the promises of God. When the Church pleads Scripture, it begins to believe in something again, and it becomes a loud-voiced Church of faith.

4. *When the Church gets passionate,* God's people are transformed into a loud-voiced Church. When God's people allow the fire of God to come over them, they start to get passionate like God's Son. When they have a passionate love for God and His Son, then the Church begins to speak with a loud voice that can shake the earth.

By nature, I am actually quite reserved. I am not normally a shouter unless I'm on a platform. However, things are changing. When we begin to get passionate about God and His love and purposes, then I believe that even the most quiet-natured among us will actually say, "Hey, there's something worth raising our voices for here! We've got something to shout from the rooftops! We believe in these living Scriptures and we are determined to make our statements of faith and cry out to the living God!"

Don't fall for the myth that says, "Life goes on whatever we do. We can't change things." I don't believe that. *Prayer changes things.* Your city can be changed if you and your fellow believers begin to respond to pressure by getting desperate, pleading Scripture, and receiving the passion of God in your lives. We need to proclaim the gospel with a new passion.

During my time at Spring Harvest in 1997, I heard the astounding testimony of Alex Buchanan, an elderly man who knows the meaning of suffering. He has suffered a number of strokes, and his wife is confined to a wheelchair with multiple sclerosis. Everything has seemed to work against them physically, yet Alex is a man who is passionate for the Lord Jesus.

He described his visit to Brownsville Assembly of God Church in Pensacola, Florida, to investigate the move of God in revival there. What impressed him the most were the great numbers of people who were coming to Christ. In a 20-month period, the staff at that church had accounted for at least 100,000 people who publicly expressed their faith in Jesus for the first time. Alex simply wanted to check it for himself because he had prayed for revival for many years.

I'll never forget the thrill I sensed surging through my spirit when Alex told us from the platform, "I can't remember the exact times, but I've been praying for revival for over 50 years" (although he then proceeded to give us the exact time, right down to the number of months, days, and hours he'd prayed). "I've been praying for all of this time," he said, "and as I sat in that Assemblies of God church in Pensacola, Florida, I realized that I was now in the place where my prayers had been answered!"

He told us, "*I was in an atmosphere of revival!* It is impossible to share exactly what was going on, but when people were asked to come to the front to respond to the gospel, people were running to the front! There were grown men who were shouting, 'Don't stop the appeal, don't stop the appeal,' as they were trying to rush to the front." One man fell to the floor and grabbed hold of Alex's leg for some reason, perhaps thinking it was a chair leg. He kept saying, "Don't let me go to hell, don't let me go to hell, don't let me go to hell!"

Alex said, "At the end of that meeting I realized I was breathing a different air than I'd ever breathed in my life. This was revival air, this is what I had prayed for, this was an outpouring of the Holy Spirit." Then he added, "I then, in a very genuine sense, prayed a similar prayer to Simeon's. When I left the meeting I said to the Lord, 'Lord, this is what I've prayed for most of my life, and I've seen it. Now let Your servant depart in peace.' "

Alex felt ready to abandon his struggle with physical infirmity and he really expected the Lord to grant his request to go home to Heaven. Evidently the Lord had another plan. Alex told us that the Lord said to him, "Alex, the answer to your prayer is, 'no.' I am not taking you home because you are going to see in the United Kingdom the things that you have seen in Pensacola, and you will see them with your own eyes."

As an Englishman, I firmly believe God's promise to Alex Buchanan. As a man of God, I also honestly believe that there are "Alex's" from virtually every country on earth who have faithfully raised their voices to God for decades, asking for revival. Now a worldwide revival stands poised to cover the earth with God's glory—if God's people will pray. I'm putting my everything on this. I believe that we are going to see a great outpouring of the Holy Spirit in the United Kingdom, in the United States and Canada, in South America, continental Europe, Africa, Australia and New Zealand, Scandinavia, Asia, the Near East, and every other nation and kingdom on earth. There is going to be a prayer surge in local churches around the world, churches filled with ordinary people like you and I. It is time for us all to get passionate about God, about His purposes, and about Jesus Christ His Son!

What Are the Effects of a Loud-Voiced Church?

Is it just that the people of God raise their voices and that it's all emotional? Are there any effects? Does anything *really* happen when the people of God raise their voices? Absolutely. I'm here to tell you that things happen with a loud-voiced Church! Now God always retains His right and prerogative to be God Almighty and to do things in His good time and in any way He chooses without our opinions or approval. However, I believe that a loud-voiced Church is going to see a number of things take place simply because they have honored God according to His Word.

1. *Prayers get answered.* In the accounts of both Ezra and Nehemiah, the people of God raised their voices to God and saw answers come from Heaven. The walls of Jerusalem that had been broken down were built again despite the best efforts of the enemies of God. The temple that was desolate was raised up again and dedicated anew to holy service. The people who had been steeped in sin openly confessed their sins and their lives were changed. They were brought back

into some semblance of order as they raised their voices, but best of all, God heard them.

In Acts 4, when the apostles and believers in Jerusalem prayed together with upraised voices, they were filled with a holy boldness and empowered by the Holy Spirit for bold witness. No, the obstacles they faced weren't removed. The pressure didn't ease off either. What happened was that God answered their prayers! A new boldness came to them and they stood for the truth in the face of death. They were free from fear and were able to continue to proclaim the name of Jesus. When the Church fervently raises its voice to Heaven in Jesus' name, prayers are answered and believers are filled with boldness. Acts 12 tells us that God dispatched an angel to supernaturally free Peter from shackles, prison gates, and scores of armed guards! Tell the negative people, "You're too late to tell me God doesn't answer prayer. He's already done it." God wants the Church of Jesus to begin to move in authority and power once again, and He wants the process to begin with the fervent prayers of a loud-voiced Church.

2. *Things get shaken.* When the Church becomes a loud-voiced Church as it did in Acts 12, things get shaken when God answers its cry.

> *After they prayed, the place where they were meeting was shaken. And they were all filled with the Holy Spirit and spoke the word of God boldly. All the believers were one in heart and mind...* (Acts 4:31-32a).

If we ever learn how to raise our voices as one Church, with one voice and one prayer of declaration, then I believe the things that hold us back can be shaken—especially the spiritual powers and principalities aligned against us. Now I don't know whether you believe in territorial spirits or dark clouds over cities, but nearly every believer will tell you he or she knows or senses that there are works of darkness that need shaking over his or her city. This will never happen simply because individuals like you or me shout and shake our fists at things. However, when the Church united, all of us together, rise up in faith; when we dare to believe that God is who He says He is; and when we declare that He is the sovereign Lord, the Lord of lords and King of kings, then things will be shaken.

3. *Prisoners get released.* When Peter landed in Herod's prison chained between two soldiers in Acts 12, he needed more than the helping hand of man. He had to somehow escape his iron shackles (he appeared to have one chain for each wrist). Then he had to pass through two sets of guards and somehow get through a massive iron gate. When God heard the cries of the Jerusalem believers, He simply sent a single angel to answer the cries of His people. That one angel shook Herod's imposing prison to its foundations and set the apostolic prisoner free. Peter could hardly believe what was happening. In fact, if you read the passage carefully, it is almost as though Peter shook himself and finally realized it was real. By that time, he found himself on the street free and clear.

The believers who were praying so intently for Peter's release also couldn't believe God's answer to their prayer when it finally arrived. They refused to believe Rhoda's report that Peter was at their door. They even started to make up these things in Acts 12:15: "It must be his angel" (which would actually take more faith to believe than it being Peter himself). The key point here is that when God's people began to pray to Him in unity as one loud voice, the prisoner was released.

4. *The impossible becomes possible.* "Well, it's impossible in our city for 80 percent of the people to come to faith in Christ. It's just not possible. It is not reasonable to expect the very climate of our city and region to be transformed." Granted, these things may be in the realm of the impossible, but we too easily forget that it is the realm of our Almighty God.

There may have been periods of history when the Church of Jesus Christ had to endure drought and dryness. But we're living in a day when God is calling us to move forward in the name of Jesus Christ, the Son of God! When God's people become a loud-voiced Church, *the impossible becomes possible*! When the people of God raise their voices together in Jesus' name, a supernatural overcoming anointing comes upon the Church.

Perhaps the most powerful Scripture passage in the Bible is found in Luke 4:18 where Jesus quotes from Isaiah 61:

The Spirit of the Lord is on Me, because He has anointed Me to preach good news to the poor. He has sent Me to proclaim freedom for the prisoners and recovery of sight for the blind, to release the oppressed, to proclaim the year of the Lord's favor (Luke 4:18-19).

In the following verses, Jesus told the people in the synagogue that day, *"Today* this scripture is fulfilled in your hearing" (Lk. 4:21b). The beauty of the gospel is this: It's *now; today* is the day of salvation; *today* is the year of the Lord's favor; *today* is the day of grace when unbelievers can come to faith in Jesus. This is our Jubilee time.

Jesus has done His part. He came and died on a cross, and then He rose from the dead to open up a new and living way back to the Presence of the Father. We need to become the loud-voiced Church that declares and believes it! This is the special time of God's favor and we are obligated to spread the news to the lost and hurting. We're living in days of the favor of God. It is the year of the Lord's favor.

Why Should the Church Raise Its Voice?

The first reason the Church should raise its voice is this: *Every member of Christ is valuable and has a contribution to make.* I believe that if we can learn to raise our voices together, God will answer our prayers and change things. He will make the impossible things possible, and He will set prisoners free. We have to break through the barrier of self-consciousness or irritation with those near us who are louder or more off-key than we are! We must break through our cultural problems and get used to hearing the voices of our fellow believers raised up to God beside and behind us. If we listen with the ears and heart of God, it will be sweet music to our ears. The importance of your prayer is what I'm talking about. Every member is valuable and has a contribution to make.

Every anointed church leader longs to see every individual in his local church get involved and be included in the purposes of God. Even though some of us are extroverts and others are introverts, we need to learn how to speak to our Father together. Anointed corporate prayer is the most economic way of praying! If we called a prayer meeting today and followed the old form of praying singly out loud, we'd be at it for hours and hours. But if we raise our voices together as one voice in one accord, we have maximized our prayer through unity. As we get used to it, we'll begin to flow in it more and more, and we'll begin to reap the rich harvest of our sown seeds of prayer as a loud-voiced Church.

The second reason we should raise our voices together in prayer is this: *The Church will raise its voice in Heaven for all eternity!* In Revelation 19:6, the apostle John tells us, "Then I heard what sounded like a great multitude, like the roar of rushing waters and like loud peals of thunder, shouting: 'Hallelujah! For our Lord God Almighty reigns.' "

I believe Heaven will resound with the heart cries of the redeemed people of God, and that those passionate cries will roar and thunder like "the sound of many waters." As far as our life in Christ right now on this plane is concerned, I believe we can hear the voice of God through the Body of Christ when it becomes the *loud-voiced Church* that cries out to God. We can get a small reflection of God's mighty voice when His people raise their voices together.

Chapter 3

Hope in the Hand of God

Revival is rooted in unity, and God is moving on His Church to bring us together in spite of ourselves. About 15 years ago on my birthday, my wife, Irene, and I were sitting down to birthday tea when I felt God say to me, "Go to Evangel Church." Now this was the local Assemblies of God, and frankly I didn't really want to go there—especially on my birthday. Nevertheless, I felt it really strongly, so I said to Irene, "I really sense I've got to go to prayer meeting over at the Assemblies of God." She simply said, "Well, you better go."

I went into this meeting and tried my best to hide in the back of the room because I didn't quite know why I'd come there. Two pastors were there that night, and one of them spotted me. "I see Brother Stuart from Lincoln Free Church is with us tonight," he said as I tried to shrink out of sight. "Come up and share with us, won't you?"

I really didn't know why I was there, and there was nothing in particular on my mind. But when I stood up, I heard myself say, "Isn't it sad that in a city of our size [it's a relatively small and compact city] that we cross by one another on our way to our groups, and we have very little fellowship with one another?" As I shared these thoughts spontaneously, I was amazed at the really good positive response coming from the people in that meeting. "You know, it's a pity that we can't do more together and just share our hearts and visions in the Lord."

At the end of the meeting, the two pastors, John Shelbourne and John Phillips, came to me and said, "We've been praying for you to come. We really sense that we should be together, but we didn't want it to look as though we were wanting to dominate or anything." Their congregation had about 300 members at the time, and the church I'd originally planted in a home had grown to about 150 people. We ended our conversation feeling that God was at least challenging us to come together in some way or another. We realized that the theory of unity among churches is good, but the practical out-working of that is a lot different. We started to pursue unity together anyway in obedience to God.

Same Language, Different Meanings

What we quickly discovered was that we spoke the same language, but we meant different things. Our ministry emphasis was different, and the guiding philosophies of the two church bodies were considerably different. Despite these things, we really felt God was causing us to come together and we started to meet together after a period of time.

To cut a long story short, we went through a short "courtship" and then came together as a new church under the name of New Life Christian Fellowship. In the short term, our strong desire to be together caused things to work quite well. After awhile, Irene and I began to feel that some of the Free Church people felt more like the other had "taken us over" rather than the two congregations joining together as equal partners. I am sure that Evangel members had similar feelings. A silent pressure seemed to build up over time, although there were never any arguments as such. Two groups eventually left the fellowship. One group that leaned toward the more radical edge and that had been with me in the home church originally felt that we had become too traditional and pulled away. Then a group that was more conservative than the main body evidently felt that they didn't want me involved, and they pulled away as well.

Although we had begun with a tremendous desire for unity, it looked as though the reverse was taking place after the "marriage." John Shelbourne, the founding pastor of the larger body, was really an evangelist—a very good evangelist. Like most evangelists, he wasn't very comfortable being tied down in church organizational structure, so he started to hand over a lot of the pastoral and organizational things to me. At that point in the transition, there just wasn't the kind of clarity at the leadership level that the church needed, and we started to experience a lot of behind-the-scenes struggles.

One day I attended a prayer conference of about 15,000 people, but all day long I felt a peculiar heaviness over me, as if there was something wrong. I just wanted to get home. When I finally got home, I learned that my oldest son, Andrew, had been rushed to the hospital for an emergency appendectomy. I thought, *Well, perhaps that's what I was feeling.* I went to the hospital to find that the operation had gone well and my son was fine, and that made me feel that everything was okay. However, as I was getting ready to go to bed, the phone rang. I was told, "John is dying. Come quickly!" By the time I entered his hospital room, John Shelbourne had already died of a heart attack at the young age of 55, with his wife Muriel at his side.

Since John had died suddenly with no warning, the next few days were devoted to overseeing what was obviously a major tragedy in the life of our young church, and especially in the lives of John's shocked family. After a period of time, one or two printed publications actually suggested that the "added pressure" created by my involvement with the church had somehow caused John's death. As preposterous as the reports sounded, they managed to make a terribly difficult situation almost unbearable for me. It was during this time that a Christian leader named Gerald Coates became a very close friend, in terms of standing with me without any strings attached. His wise counsel and unwavering friendship became a major support to Irene and me during those difficult days. He has continued to make himself available to us and we owe him a great deal.

Two Sticks in the Hand of Man

Eventually the church began to pull together in united grief, and things started to go quite well. We even began to grow again. I now was clearly overseeing the thing, but there were never any noticeable problems between myself and John's widow, Muriel, or his sons. Yet there was an unspoken distance between us that couldn't be defined. I just didn't know what they really thought about me. Despite our best efforts, the two church bodies were like the "two sticks" in the Book of Ezekiel that God wanted to make one.

I heard a friend of mine named Jack Groblewski speak on this story during a church conference, but I revamped it after experiencing the hand of God in this area. The story of the two sticks is found in Ezekiel 37:

> *The word of the Lord came to me: "Son of man, take a stick of wood and write on it, 'Belonging to Judah and the Israelites associated with him.' Then take another stick of wood,*

*and write on it, 'Ephraim's stick, belonging to Joseph and all the house of Israel associated with him.' Join them together into one stick so that they will become one in your hand. When your countrymen ask you, 'Won't you tell us what you mean by this?' say to them, 'This is what the Sovereign Lord says: I am going to take the stick of Joseph—which is in Ephraim's hand—and of the Israelite tribes associated with him, and join it to Judah's stick, making them a single stick of wood, and **they will become one in My hand.'** Hold before their eyes the sticks you have written on and say to them, 'This is what the Sovereign Lord says: I will take the Israelites out of the nations where they have gone. I will gather them from all around and bring them back into their own land. **I will make them one nation in the land,** on the mountains of Israel. There will be one king over all of them and they will never again be two nations or be divided into two kingdoms' "* (Ezekiel 37:15-22).

This is a picture of divine unity created from human diversity. Those of us who have longed for unity in the Church have often found that division comes on the heels of any drive or process toward unity. Historically, when God has breathed the new life of renewal or revival on the Church, the unity that I believe is in the heart of God has sadly been missing from the lives of key church leaders and church organizations.

The first part of Ezekiel 37 contains the prophet's vision of the valley of dry bones and the story of how God breathed His life and power into a broken and deserted people. This has been one of the most graphic pictures of revival in the Bible through the years. An often overlooked point is that any time the breath of God comes, it brings a rattling and shaking with it. The wind of the Spirit always disturbs the existing spiritual and natural landscape. There is always disturbance in revival, but out of this shaking and rattling come divine form and substance.

In every major move of God's Spirit, His will has been for men to go beyond the rattling and the shaking stage to a place of divine unity and structure. After the bones in Ezekiel's vision were reunited, given life, and transformed into a mighty army, the focus of the prophet turned to *maintaining the divine Presence*. Any time God breathes on us in His power, it is vitally important that we then *take hold of that life and power, and move forward in unity*.

Obedience Allows God to Take Over

Throughout the passage in Ezekiel 37, the hand of God is of critical importance. Not only was the hand of God upon the prophet Ezekiel, but God's hand also was the site of total transformation and supernatural joining. Yes, the hand of the prophet was important, but his role was primarily one of obedience, not power. When the man of God obeyed, God Himself took the two sticks in His hand to miraculously make them one.

You have probably gathered by now that I feel very strongly on this issue of unity. All too often, the power and life of God in the Church have been dissipated through needless division and strife over personal issues. The second part of Ezekiel 37 paints a prophetic picture of unity that is vital to the move of God in this generation. Notice that the miracle begins with two sticks in the hands of man. Each stick bore a "label" or human identification that had become symbolic of division rather than unity. Very often we organize our church life under "tribal banners" of historic or traditional identification, theological concepts, personal ownership, or family loyalties. We proudly say, "This stick belongs to me. This church belongs to me. This ministry belongs to me. This is my stick because it's got my name on it!"

God wasn't happy with these two self-styled "nations" sticking to their respective side of the north/south line, and doing their own thing. He had sovereignly created them as vital parts of one nation before sin entered the picture. As usually happens in these situations, each "stick group" or kingdom became tragically limited in scope and destiny. They had fallen far short of God's best.

These two tribes had been independent from one another for years, and their independence gradually turned into outright rivalry and feuding. Matthew Henry, the Bible commentator writing at the dawn of the eighteenth century, said, "They had been two sticks crossing and thwarting one another, nay, beating and bruising one another...."[1] After ten years of exile with Jerusalem destroyed, the people had given up hope. Their nation was dying. These two kingdoms had tried unsuccessfully to come back together for centuries. They were designed to be together but remained hopelessly separated by their differences.

Ezekiel, an unknown prophet at the time, was sent to prophetically portray the miracle God was about to work in these feuding groups who were unable to help themselves. In our day, God has said powerful and great things to us concerning this great move of renewal and revival, and *we are unable to bring these things to pass in our own strength.*

The first thing God did was to command the man Ezekiel to grasp the two sticks in his hands and label them with their respective symbols of division and private loyalty. Then the prophet was told to hold the sticks together in his hand for the people to *see.* We have accepted the idea that there will always be division in the Church of Jesus, but the Scriptures teach otherwise. Jesus even prayed otherwise in His high priestly prayer. Three times He prayed we might be one, and that the world would take notice of our unity and give the glory to God (see Jn. 17:11,21-22). Now either this unity message is "pie in the sky," or it is a prayer that God the Father is out to answer for God the Son!

The only way God's Presence in revival will impact cities, towns, and entire regions is if the local churches comprising the Church of Jesus Christ come together to stand in unity around one banner—the banner of the risen Christ. That means we will have to lay aside our private agendas and individualistic banners of private loyalty. When the King calls, all men lay aside their local thinking to answer the royal summons. We need to be willing to say, "I am the King's man. I am the King's woman. We are the King's Church, united under the banner of the Lamb and Lion."

Of course we all have our individual and corporate identities, but the central issue is the Lordship of Christ. God has bigger plans for your local church than for it to merely exist as a lone stick marked with some private name and exclusive loyalty. God has called His prophets to again lift high the many sticks signifying our division so we can see how isolated we are. The Lord is calling us to place our many sticks into His hand so He can supernaturally blend us into one stick under the banner of His Son.

Unity Releases the Anointing

I believe there is a direct link between this call to unity and the intensity and depth of the anointing of the Holy Spirit that we are seeing today. Unity in the Body of Christ is synonymous with the holy anointing oil symbolic of God's anointing. There is a call upon the Church of Jesus Christ to discard the extreme independence and possessiveness that causes us to taunt one another with statements like, "This stick is mine and that stick is yours." God wants to replace that fleshly provincial thinking with a bigger prophetic vision of unity straight from His Father's heart. The Church needs to rediscover the truth that *unity releases God's anointing.*

God delights in calling each of us (and our local church bodies) by name, but He is *not* delighted when we lift our individual identities and local agendas higher than His direct command that we be one! I don't know about you, but I don't want to be part of a stick or fellowship that is held solely in the hands of mere men. I want to be able to declare with Ezekiel, "The hand of the Lord was upon me" (Ezek. 37:1a).

Something has to shift in our thinking and our actions. We need to move away from blindly pursuing *our* will, *our* way, *our* agenda, and *our* way of seeing things. We need to tie in with God's vision of something far bigger and more glorious—a vision of a supernatural Church noted for its remarkable unity with diversity, a Church that manifests the glory of the Lord to the lost world.

A miracle happened in Ezekiel 37:19 when the two competing sticks in the hand of man became one stick in the hand of God! The Lord designed one Church to operate with allegiance to only one Head, the Lord Jesus Christ. Of course the Body of Christ will display diversity in its unity, but God is looking for *one stick* composed of many sticks joined together in His hand in this generation.

Characteristics of the One-Stick Church

There are four things we need to notice about the "one stick" Church:

1. *Unity only happens when God's people see and listen to His vision of what they can become.* In Ezekiel 37:20-21, God says, "Hold before their *eyes* the sticks you have written on and *say* to them, 'This is what the Sovereign

Lord says....' " The Old Testament prophets often used or literally became living visual aids to help people see what God was saying. In verse 20 quoted above, God was literally telling Ezekiel, "Fill their eyes with this...."

God has not called us to independence, but to obedience and unity. Somehow we have to fill our eyes with the heavenly possibility of *unity in the Church* in our cities, regions, and nations. It is the very vision and command of God. He has raised up wonderful models of this miracle in Argentina and Brazil where hundreds of churches and leaders have exchanged their local banners of vision for God's vision of entire nations united under His Son. God is telling His leaders around the world to proclaim to His people, "Fill your eyes with this! Look at the potential of unity in My people around the world. Look at the possibilities of a unified Kingdom under Jesus!" This would literally qualify us for the blessings and anointing described in Psalm 133.

Most of us in the Church know that we're meant to walk in unity with our brothers and sisters. We also know we need unity in each local flock of God, but we find it hard to go beyond mere theory to genuine reality. We always seem to end up shouting at one another, "But this stick belongs to me!" Even in the context of a local Christian fellowship or church, you will generally find many different gifts, abilities, and visions residing together, hopefully under one unified corporate vision. We need to hold the vision of "one stick" before one another constantly while encouraging one another, "Fill your eyes with the possibilities of us all walking together, living together, and dwelling together in unity." We should no longer say, "This is my stick" or "This is my ministry." We must begin to declare, "We are God's stick and God's ministry."

It is God's delight to take broken down, deserted, and isolated things in His hands and make them one stick, right before our eyes.

So often we say, "This is my stick, this is my patch, this is mine," but God says, "Put it in My hands and two can become one." If you've given up hope on seeing certain relationships reconciled and healed, do not let go of your vision. In the hands of God, the impossible becomes possible. There's a better way than extreme independence, there's a better way than doing your own thing, there's a better thing than just having a stick with your name on it. That way is to sink everything you have and everything you are into the larger purposes of God. He has one Church and one vision for this world: to see the world saved and brought to the Savior.

2. *Two sticks into one is no "celestial trick or a sleight of hand."* The more cynical among us are inclined to stop the prophet or spokesman preaching unity to say, "Hey, wait a minute. You're holding two sticks, but we know that underneath your hand the sticks are still broken. This is just a little trick, isn't it? This is just some kind of feel-good gimmick to help the people feel better."

God isn't interested in pulling a magician's trick to create some kind of cosmetic togetherness that is doomed to ultimately fall apart again. God has commanded us to hold up our sticks so He can *lay His hand on us and make us one.* God is looking for a people who will pay the price of obedience to walk in unity in their city, in their region, in their nation, and in the world. God is after genuine unity in the midst of diversity, not empty platitudes accompanied by meaningless smiles and hurried hugs at the end of meetings. He dreams of a Bride, a Church, that lives, dwells, and ministers together in unity under the hand of God.

Even the best of local church families experiences the ups and downs common to any marriage, but God wants us to walk in committed relationship so we can go beyond where we are. He wants us to become the prophetic people He is calling us to be. Something bigger and greater needs to take place in our cities and nations, and it will only come to pass as we walk *together* in unity.

God is looking for a people who will be empowered, who will be willing to sink their own little initiative into the greater and grander purposes of God. God is wanting us to be part of the whole. God is after a unity that is more than skin-deep. We need to be able to disagree while still loving one another. Unity is not about everybody agreeing with everyone else. It has to do with the heart of God that *beats for unity*.

> 3. *Our union is hidden in His hand.* God may begin the miracle process by lifting our divided parts before our eyes through the human hands of His servants, but the end of the matter is solely in His hands! The warning and the vision may come to us through human means at God's command, but the miracle of unity comes under God's hand! God has His purposes for us, and He wants our unity to be hidden in His grasp, in His hands.

There are various stages to unity where man is concerned. The first you could call *confederacy*. In a confederacy, everybody joins together because they need one another. Once the perceived need or danger passes, the confederacy will dissolve.

The second stage or level of unity is *amalgamation*. This describes a new substance or entity formed by mixture. Very often we see this kind of mixture in church life, sometimes for the good and sometimes for the worse.

God is looking for more than confederacy or amalgamation. He's looking for union. That means we have to lay down our "sticks" and private initiatives so we can lift up the one stick of Jesus Christ.

4. *God's hand is the hand of anointed leadership.* Ezekiel the prophet was just an ordinary man. But God was saying, "You are My representative and prophet. You are doing My will when you take these sticks and hold them high in your hand before the people."

How can unity come to pass in the broken and divided Church we see today? God can do anything, but He always prefers to use the hands of men in the process. The final miracle can only come from Him, but He has chosen to use flawed and very human people to accomplish His will among men. That means again that we have to believe that He is big enough to cover for and regulate the weaknesses of our spiritual leaders in the Church. (It seems like it always gets back to faith in the Lordship of Jesus, doesn't it? Jack, I hope I've done your message justice!)

During my difficult times in the months after John Shelbourne's death, I didn't know it but God was about to totally change the heart and call of New Life Fellowship. He was about to make the two sticks one just as He did in Ezekiel's day.

Muriel's Miracle on the Floor

The renewal came to England in 1994, and shortly after its arrival I was deeply impacted by the Presence of God. That was when Muriel Shelbourne phoned and said, "Will you come and pray with me?"

I took another pastor from the fellowship and we prayed with Muriel in her home. Nothing dramatic happened at the time, but she did say that for the next 24 hours she consistently wanted to kneel. The impulse was so strong that she kept getting out of bed and kneeling throughout the night. I was genuinely pleased that Muriel was being blessed, but I was troubled over the fact that I had never been particularly close to the family. I knew there were still some hidden questions about the history of our church merger and the past in general.

During a Tuesday night "refreshing" meeting, Muriel began to exhibit some very strange behavior after receiving prayer. Irene and I decided to go over and see what was going on. Muriel was lying on the floor and making really strange sounds. It sounded like she was calling something. She kept saying something like, "Cooie, cooie!" She also had placed her hands inside her shoes and kept banging them on the floor. I couldn't help but think to myself, *What's going on here?*

To all outward appearances, Muriel Shelbourne was doing some very silly things. How many people in their right mind have you seen banging on the floor with their shoes on their hands while making odd "cooie" sounds? It would have been easier to simply dismiss Muriel's actions as something demonic, but I knew her well enough to exercise caution. We could easily end up cursing what God wanted to bless!

This went on for quite awhile, but after about 20 minutes, Muriel opened her eyes and saw Irene and myself. Then she began making those peculiar sounds again, and called out, "Cooie, cooie. I'm coming home, I'm coming home!" Then she got up.

I didn't know what was going on, but obviously God was blessing her, so I thought nothing more of it until the following Sunday when she came to me and said, "The most remarkable thing happened to me last Tuesday. It's perhaps the most amazing thing that's ever happened to me in my life. Can I share it?" I said "yes" and hoped I'd done the right thing.

When Muriel came to the front, she brought along a plastic bag containing some gumsole boots (we call them Wellington boots). Then she said, "I've got to share with you, *my spiritual family*, about something God did." Muriel had everyone's attention because she had never talked like this before.

First Muriel described what had happened on Tuesday night, and then she began to explain what was really happening on the inside as she lay on the floor. She said the Holy Spirit took her back to her childhood, to the time when she was 10 or 11 years old. Muriel was brought up in a Welsh mining village, and every day she had to walk through a densely wooded area to catch a school bus on the other side.

She had developed a little ritual for her passage through the woods, since she often had to cross muddy ground during the walk to the bus. Her parents would often say, "Now Muriel, you need to put your boots on as you walk through the woods. Then you can put your shoes back on once you reach the other side." So Muriel followed this little ritual every day, and when she returned on the school bus at the end of the day, she'd reverse the process.

The problem was that when she came back through the woods each evening, she often felt very nervous either because of the coming darkness or because of just feeling alone. That led her to develop a unique calling sound to alert her parents that she was coming through the woods on her way home: "Cooie, cooie! I'm coming home!"

She Relived the Loss of Her Father

When the Holy Spirit took her back to her childhood, she felt as though she was going through those familiar woods again. This happened two times that Tuesday night. During her first trip through the woods, she said she felt like she was going through a bereavement over the death of her father. Muriel apparently lost her father while she was very young, and during her Spirit-led trip through the woods of her childhood, she once again felt the searing pain of losing her dad while she was so young.

As she walked through this woods, she somehow sensed that she was calling out to God, "Cooie, cooie! I'm coming home," and tapping her boots together as she had done as a child. As soon as she emerged from the woods, she felt that God had brought deep healing and wholeness to her concerning her feelings for her father.

Then the scene changed again, and Muriel found herself coming through the woods a second time. This time she felt she was carrying the bereavement of her husband, with all the darkness and the pain her loss brought to her. This time, as she came through the woods, she was calling out as before, but not to her father (he used to meet her while calling out her name).

Here's Your New Dad

Muriel said she could remember coming through the woods, and in her thinking, she was calling out for her father, but when she opened her eyes, she immediately saw Irene and myself. Now there is a bit of a difference in our ages, but Muriel said that as she came through the woods in the vision calling out, "Cooie, cooie. I'm coming home!" and looked directly at Irene and myself, the Holy Spirit said, "This man can be trusted. He's your new dad."

Muriel shared this story with the church on Father's Day of 1995, the exact day that the glory of God suddenly descended on the congregation of Brownsville Assembly of

God Church in Pensacola, Florida. After she shared her experience under the hand of God, she publicly gave me a Father's Day card that said, "To my new spiritual dad."

From that moment in time, every "question mark" about our role in the local fellowship evaporated. Muriel Shelbourne is my biggest supporter (and I think Irene and I are her biggest fans too). In one brief moment of time, God sovereignly answered every question about our history as two congregations called to be one. They were simply swallowed up in God's hand.

In that moment in time, not only was there a joining of individual sticks in the congregation, but I also can honestly say that we were joined together as one congregation too. We suddenly began to experience a oneness and a unity that we had never had before. It was just fantastic. Since then, Muriel has shared her story in more than a hundred Assemblies of God in Great Britain, and all of them have been impacted by the renewal.

Characteristics of One Stick

Any time two or more sticks are joined together in the hand of God, you should see at least four characteristics that you will not find in independent sticks.

1. The first characteristic of the one unified stick is *moral integrity*, or *holiness*. God said in Ezekiel 37:23, "They will no longer defile themselves with their idols and vile images or with any of their offenses, for I will save them from all their sinful backsliding, and I will cleanse them...."

When the hand of God is upon the Church, things will change. God is calling us to be a holy people. We may struggle with the old life and the implications of what God is calling us to. However, when we come under the hand of God, it becomes possible for us to walk in integrity and holiness before Him. As one of our Youth for Christ workers put it, "God is getting very choosy at the moment."

We're living in days of an outpouring of the Holy Spirit, and that carries responsibilities with it. If God's breath causes me to rattle and shake on the floor and laugh, then there are lasting responsibilities with that. Unless the touch of God brings genuine change in my life, then I am offending the One who lived and died for me. When the stick comes together in the hand of God, something quite remarkable starts to happen. His righteousness is not only imputed to us (assigned though we have not earned it), but it is *imparted* or transferred to us as well.

I'm expecting to be a better father through this outpouring of God's Presence. I'm expecting to be a better husband and to live a purer life. God's spotlight is upon us today. When we come under His hand, there should be an impartation of His righteousness that makes us want to end our backbiting and gossip. Moral integrity and holiness are characteristics of anointed ministers in a stick that's under the hand of God.

2. A unified stick under God's hand should enjoy a *secure relationship* with God. The Lord said in the Book of Ezekiel:

> *...And I will cleanse them. They will be My people, and I will be their God. My servant David will be king over them, and they will all have one shepherd. They will follow My laws and be careful to keep My decrees. ... My dwelling place will be with them; I will be their God, and they will be My people. Then the nations will*

know that I the Lord make Israel holy, when My sanctuary is among them forever (Ezekiel 37:23-24,27-28).

3. Another characteristic of a unified stick in God's Kingdom is *obedient trust*. Ezekiel 37:24b says, "They will follow My laws and be careful to keep My decrees." Obedience should flow at this stage of unity under God's hand. Jesus Christ is the Head of the Church. Once we submit to Him, we will begin to manifest the characteristic obedient trust in the Lord and His Word as we live under His rule and Lordship.

4. The final characteristic of the unified stick under God's hand is found in Psalm 133 as well as in Ezekiel 37:26: *promised blessing*. God said, "I will make a covenant of peace with them; it will be an everlasting covenant. I will establish them and increase their numbers, and I will put My sanctuary among them forever" (Ezek. 37:26).

In Psalm 133, God commands a blessing on those who dwell together in unity. God longs to command this blessing upon His Church as we come under the hand of God and Christ's rule. My prayer is that we as a Church united will say:

We acknowledge that we've been given a stick with our name on it, but we want to sink that stick into God's greater purposes and keep it under the hand of God.

We want our Father to use us as an implement of His grace and glory in this generation. We put His vision before our eyes and fill our vision with His desire—it's better to be together than alone; it's better to walk in harmony than to walk apart. We say, as Jesus taught us to pray, "Not our will, but Yours be done. Not 'my' stick, Lord, but our stick under Your hand, hidden in union with You."

Endnote

1. Matthew Henry, *Matthew Henry's Commentary on the Whole Bible* (Welwyn, England: Evangelical Press, 1982), excerpt from commentary on Ezekiel 37:22.

Chapter 4

Hear the Lion's Roar!

Everything in the meeting seemed to go smoothly until I told the 30 or so pastors from Pittsburgh, Pennsylvania, about Muriel's vision of the woods. (I am rarely able to share her story in public without being driven to tears.) When I reached the point where Muriel Shelbourne was calling out for her father and opened her eyes and saw Irene and I, a prominent African-American pastor named Joseph Garlington began to weep. Instantly, the whole group of church leaders began to weep under a deep intercessory burden for the wounds over their city and their multiracial congregations.

I learned later that much of Pastor Garlington's ministry has been devoted to the biblical mandate for reconciliation between races and the many factions of the Church. I had been ministering on the themes of unity and reconciliation when I shared Muriel's story, and all of a sudden Joseph, whom I didn't know at the time, suddenly started sobbing. When he heard Muriel's story about her childhood pain, his heart broke all over again. Very quickly, nearly every leader in that room fell to their faces sobbing and crying out to God. It was a major, major move of the Spirit.

I had come to Pittsburgh at the invitation of my friends, Bill and Melinda Fish, who pastor a thriving church in that city. By the time I got there, the power of God had already broken out in a number of the churches in the city, so I was asked to lead some joint renewal meetings. Rather than ministering in one church, I found myself facing a racially mixed crowd of hundreds of Christians from many different churches and denominations including Episcopalians, Pentecostals, Methodists, Baptists, and non-denominational churches. I shared the story of God's work in my life and the church in England, and then we had an extended time of ministry that went into the early morning hours.

The outpouring of God's Presence came the next day during this special meeting for the leaders of the various churches. Within moments after the sobbing broke out, the Presence of God suddenly descended on the place and the leaders began to repent to one another (between sobs) about wrong attitudes and grievances they had held against one another. Afterwards, Joseph Garlington told me that we needed to continue with the meetings. He felt that God had sent me and that I shouldn't go home yet. It was then early December, and the leaders wanted me to stay until Christmas! So I stayed on another week and led meetings every night, and a powerful excitement began to course through the various churches across Pittsburgh.

After I returned to England, the Pittsburgh meetings continued until Christmas. In early January, the leaders in Pittsburgh phoned me again to ask if I would return to the States again to take part in a 40-day series of meetings. I went back a second time, but this time I took my wife, Irene, along. This was the first time I had seen a truly *citywide* move of God in the United States. God was impacting many churches at the same time, not just one or two. Throughout the 40-day period, the churches were meeting together for prayer and fasting. Afterward, they continued to hold a weekly interdenominational leader's meeting.

The Weight of Tough Criticism

This kind of citywide outpouring has happened in many places in Argentina, but it was almost unprecedented at the time in the U.S. The movement in Pittsburgh subsequently began to struggle under the weight of tough criticism from sources outside the outpouring, and many of the churches wavered under the attack.

The striking thing about the move of God in Pittsburgh was that it was ignited when the church leaders heard about God's compassion and provision for Muriel's crushing pain over the untimely losses of her husband and father. The Scriptures are filled with instances where God is moved to action and declaration over the suffering of mankind. As I have talked with Joseph Garlington and Bill and Melinda Fish, we all felt that we were on the verge of a very significant move of God at that time in Pittsburgh. We are also convinced that God has far more in store for that city.

God is working intimately in people's lives, and I think we have no idea just how fiercely His heart burns for His people when He hears their cries of pain and longing. Another great story from those days in Pittsburgh concerned a young African-American woman who received prayer during those meetings. Some people were watching her with apprehension because she cried and sobbed for about 20 minutes, and for the next 20 minutes laughed uncontrollably. Fortunately there was a wise counselor nearby who wasn't content to simply watch the woman and dismiss her outward behavior as mere emotionalism. She went to the trouble to ask the young woman what was going on while she was on the floor.

Black Shoes and Rejection

This young lady said, "When I was prayed for, the Lord seemed to take me back to my childhood. I was brought up in a poor Roman Catholic family, and the Lord reminded me of the day I went to Mass for my first confirmation. Unfortunately, my parents couldn't afford to buy me the new white dress and white shoes normally purchased for the occasion. They managed to buy me a new white dress, but they just couldn't afford the new shoes, so I had to wear the black shoes I normally wore every day." The rejection that this woman felt as a little girl forced to stand out from the rest of the children during her first confirmation Mass burned a lasting scar into her delicate spirit.

She said that as she lay on the floor, the Lord gently reminded her of this long-forgotten incident. She relived all of the pain she felt when she was mistreated and ridiculed by her peers at school because her parents couldn't afford the proper shoes. When the pain rose up in her, she began to cry and weep bitterly over the years she had carried this secret pain and rejection from such a seemingly insignificant thing.

The counselor told her, "I understand why you were crying, but what happened when the tears turned to laughter?" The young woman smiled and said, "While I was crying and feeling all that pain flow through me, I had a vision of Jesus. He walked toward me, and He was wearing a long white gown. As soon as He got close to me, He silently lifted the bottom of the gown off of the floor, and I suddenly noticed that He had black shoes on His feet!" Once again she was engulfed in a wave of joy and laughter. The Lord went to incredible lengths to let this precious sister know that He was personally identifying with her pain and her hurts, and suddenly everything was made right again.

That in itself is a fantastic testimony about God's intimate concern for our personal hurts and suffering, but there's more. I ministered at the Spring Harvest gathering in England about 18 months later in April of 1997. As you recall from my earlier comments, I had been asked to help out in the special "refreshing" meetings offered late in the evenings for anyone in that predominately non-Charismatic gathering who was interested in the outpouring or renewal of the Spirit. I was really determined to think of a story that might disarm the built-in defensiveness of the people about outward manifestations. I wanted to help them to see that when God touches someone, something happens internally; and that they shouldn't merely look at the outward appearance of things.

He's Going to Mention the Shoes

I decided to share this story about the lady's black shoes at confirmation to help them look beyond the outside to see God's real work within, and things seemed to go well. The next day, a black woman came up to me and said, "An amazing thing happened to me last night. I decided to come to the refreshing meeting to observe what was going on, but because I'm a Roman Catholic, I really wasn't planning to get any prayer. I had heard about some of the things you were experiencing and I wanted to see them for myself. But as I was coming in, I prayed to God, 'If this is for me, let there be something shared that will put my mind at ease, so I'll know it's You.'

"When you started to share about the lady in Pittsburgh, I told myself, 'I think he's going to mention the shoes.' " At that point I just had to interrupt her: "What do you mean?"

She said, "Well, I was brought up in a Roman Catholic home, and my parents were poor. At my first confirmation, my parents couldn't afford any white shoes either, so they *painted* my black shoes white. When you mentioned the black shoes, I knew God was talking to me and I was touched by the Spirit."

What are the odds of two people—one in Pittsburgh and one in England—with the same story and the same pain receiving healing from God? I am amazed at the intimacy God demonstrates by His Spirit as He works intricately in people's lives around the world. It's fantastic.

The two issues of unity and reconciliation in the Church are closely linked to God's intimate love and care for His people. I saw God sweep across widely diverse groups of people throughout 1997 with a compelling spirit of reconciliation and unity. The power of the thing was astounding. First I saw it blaze up in those meetings with Joseph Garlington and the people in Pittsburgh. I also saw God's Presence affect a mixed crowd of Protestants and Roman Catholics gathered for a historic meeting in Belfast, Northern Ireland! I was invited to Belfast in 1996 by Paul Reid, the leader of a large church there. He arranged to have the meetings in a large leisure center, and about 800 people came.

I spoke to the mixed crowd of Roman Catholics and Protestants from the biblical story of Joseph and his brothers found in the Book of Genesis. Throughout the meeting, and particularly during the ministry time at the end, a deep sobbing burst out across a number of the congregation that brought incredible depths of healing to ancient wounds as people felt God's desire to bring reconciliation and unity among His people in Ireland. God did a mighty work in Belfast that is still bearing good fruit.

I'm excited over the things God is doing across the earth today. The prophetic signs indicate that we are in the midst of one of the greatest moves of God in human history. I've been in meetings where there was such a deep awareness of the Presence of God that nearly every person present began to release deep groanings and experience a kind of anguish, almost as if they were bearing a burden or bringing something to birth. (I think there's a scriptural foundation for this phenomenon. Paul talks about intercession and groanings that cannot be expressed in Romans 8:26. The Scriptures often speak of burdens, weights, or concerns carried by the servants of God.)

When Men Roar Like Lions

I've seen people who were very educated and normally very conservative begin to act as though they were in pain during revival meetings. When asked about it later, they often explain that they sensed God was bringing something to birth and were simply caught up in the spiritual labor coming through the work of the Holy Spirit. I've also been in meetings where the power of God was very evident, in which I saw people who had proven prophetic gifts begin to groan and even roar like a lion!

You may have heard of the controversy over the "animal sounds" and other manifestations that sometimes appear in renewal or revival meetings. We should avoid getting so tied up with analytical criticism of unusual outward phenomenon that we miss some very vital message that God wants to pass to His Church. God uses His people to carry things from the spirit realm to the natural, and invariably our weak flesh will react in unusual ways when faced with the unusual power of His manifest Presence.

Sometimes the Lord imparts signs of His anguish over the suffering of innocents, and at other times He manifests a sign of His judgments that are brought prophetically to the Church.

We need to be watching for these things, but we should never judge something solely by outward appearances.

This phenomenon of roaring like a lion particularly intrigued me. I knew of many people who would write off such manifestations as pure emotionalism or outright oddities, but I sensed that there was something more to this—something deeper and holier than any of us understood. My research led me to the Book of Amos and the roar of the Lion of Judah.

Blessed to Bless

God is raising our faith expectations today. People around the world are beginning to believe that there is perhaps a great outpouring of the Holy Spirit just around the corner, a move of God that will bring many people into the Kingdom of God in a great harvest. At the same time, we face a terrible danger that could quickly quench the move of God in our generation: We could become *ingrown*. Every great move of God has faced the hidden temptation of becoming "inward looking," and most have succumbed to it. This happens when we become so engrossed with receiving and being blessed, with laughing or crying, and with falling down under the power, that we stop thinking about taking the light of God's Presence into the darkness. We may very well miss the very plan and purpose of God for this revival if we refuse to take the things God is doing among us out to the lost and dying world around us! We *must* allow the fruits of God's prophetic activity among us, with the passionate prayer and divine visitation, to "spill over" to the harvest field. We have no right to insist on keeping it all to ourselves.

God blesses and refreshes His people specifically to *equip and empower them* to share His glory and love in the earth! Our generation lives in an age characterized on the one hand by a great and growing darkness of sin, and on the other hand by the intensifying light of God's glory. Even the unchurched can tell you "the dark is getting darker." Spend five minutes with a newspaper or a television news program and you will quickly agree.

On the other hand, when I think of the unprecedented spiritual hunger and the thirst I see in people and churches around the world, I am reassured that the Almighty God is at work! I am also keenly aware that Jesus Christ is calling all of us to take our place beside Him, the Great Intercessor, and to take up the challenge of prayer today. He has given us a mandate to pray with prophetic insight and anointing to invade every area of darkness with His unquenchable light.

God wants us to take up the cause of the broken, the downcast, the forgotten, and the discarded people in the world. He wants to see us begin to speak out with new understanding and compassion for the plight of those unable to help themselves. He also wants us to bear the light of Jesus Christ into our workplaces and schoolrooms. He wants us to shine with His glory in every place we work and live.

God Takes People Seriously

God's heart hurts for people. He longs to see people turn to Christ. Jesus said, "For God so loved the world that He gave His one and only Son, that whoever believes in Him shall not perish but have eternal life" (Jn. 3:16). God loves people, and it goes all the way back to the beginning.

In Genesis 1:27, the Bible says, "So God created man in His own image, in the image of God He created him; male and female He created them." God takes people seriously because they were created to carry the very image of God. God loves people.

While reading through the Book of Amos, which most people are quick to admit is one of the more "difficult" books in the Bible, I suddenly realized that Amos was picturing much of what is happening in the Church today. Amos the prophet was called to proclaim a number of very unpopular truths to his generation. He warned that God was about to judge certain Gentile nations, and that He was going to judge Judah and the people of God as well. This prophet also brought a message of great hope in God's grace and forgiveness and prophesied of the day God's people would be given a land with prosperity and blessing.

> ..."**The Lord roars from Zion** and thunders from Jerusalem; the pastures of the shepherds dry up, and the top of Carmel withers." ... **The lion has roared**—who will not fear? **The Sovereign Lord has spoken**—who can but prophesy? (Amos 1:2; 3:8).

Amos reminds us of something many Christians and unsaved people want to forget: God judges people and nations. The thing that amazed me the most was *what* God judges. Amos tells us that God judges nations and individuals for *the way they treat other people*. As we enter the twenty-first century, Amos is warning us anew that *God takes people very seriously*.

Amos has described a picture of God as a lion who has roared. A hunting lion roars just before it pounces on its prey. God is beginning to roar in anger over the things He sees. He is about to judge.

There is a small Hebrew phrase that appears on a number of occasions in Amos the prophet's lists of offenses triggering God's judgment. This phrase is, "For three sins...even for four, I will not turn back." It appears *five times* in Amos chapter 1 and *three times* in chapter 2.

God's judgment builds slowly because, as His Word declares, He is slow to become angry (see Ps. 145:8). However, when God's anger is finally kindled, it is always just and deserved (unlike man's). We, on the other hand, often get angry very quickly and easily, and we almost always regret our anger later.

The Book of Amos describes how God's judgment on various nations continued to build as those nations sinned once, and then sinned a second time, and then a third. As the sinning grew worse, the nations finally crossed the line of God's grace and mercy. There comes a time when the Lion of Judah judges. There comes a time when God says, "Enough is enough." The God who is slow to anger, the Lion of Righteousness, has begun to roar—one, two, three times, and even a fourth time. Then the judgment comes.

As I went through the things these condemned nations had done, I was amazed at the things God takes seriously. First of all, I noticed that God didn't bring judgment for the things I thought He would! It was almost as if God wasn't as concerned about man's sins against Him as He was about their sins against one another!

God is personally interested in the way we treat our spouses and our children. He is *very serious* about it! We may be surprised at how sternly and seriously God will judge nations for how they treat people under their authority. I want us to examine some of the judgments described by Amos the prophet so you will see just how angry God becomes when He sees people being abused and treated unfairly.

There are three major things that make God roar as the Judge of all flesh, the Lion of Judah, and the Defender of the meek:

1. **The Lion roars when we treat people as things and objects.**

Amos the prophet declared that God's judgment was coming to Damascus because of Syria's violent mistreatment of the Jews as things and objects.

God will judge excessive violence and hatred in warfare. "This is what the Lord says: 'For three sins of Damascus, even for four, I will not turn back my wrath. Because she threshed Gilead with sledges having iron teeth' " (Amos 1:3). God condemned several Gentile nations for violence beyond the norm. He was not blind to their bloodletting, their hatred, and their cruel warfare against other nations.

We all need to remember that God sees every single act of hatred and violence, and the day will come when the Lion roars. Edom incurred God's wrath for this kind of sin as well. God said, "...I will not turn back My wrath. Because he pursued his brother with a sword, stifling all compassion, because his anger raged continually and his fury flamed unchecked" (Amos 1:11). Gaza was condemned "because she took captive whole communities and sold them to Edom" (Amos 1:6b).

Even in our so-called "civilized" age, there are nations and societies treating certain people like "commodities" to be bought and sold, abused, or simply eliminated in cold blood if they are deemed a threat to their private agendas. Thousands of people—including Christians and Christian missionaries—are being treated violently and shamefully even as you read these words. It is time for the Church to rise up with a prophetic response from God's heart—we need to roar out God's indignation over the mistreatment of the helpless and the weak, and of those He has dispatched to serve them.

The Lion roars when women are violated and unborn babies are pulled from the womb. Women, children, and the unborn are not things or objects to be abused, misused, or aborted at will. Some of the most violent and brutal sins that have ignited

God's consuming anger concern acts of violence against the unborn and motherhood. Amos 1:13 says, "...For three sins of Ammon, even for four, I will not turn back My wrath. Because he ripped open the pregnant women of Gilead in order to extend his borders."

This is a horrific picture of warfare—a portrait of violence sure to earn God's deadly wrath and judgment. Yet it is uncomfortably close to home in England and the United States as well as many other so-called enlightened societies where the wholesale abortion of living children is the "law of the land."

Although most of these countries claim to live in freedom and safety, one of the most dangerous places to live on the face of the earth is in the mother's womb. The wombs of women are being forced open and millions of babies are being slaughtered every month by abortionists in the world's top Western societies (although even this sordid slaughterhouse operation doesn't compare to that of Communist-ruled China where the number of slaughtered *full-term* babies rivals the gruesome pre-term harvest of death in the West).

I have to be honest here. I'm not plugging for any political office or promoting any agenda but God's agenda. God declared it in His Word: *When the lives of babies are taken in violence, the Lion roars.* No thinking Christian who knows the Bible can help but understand that God's wrath is growing as thousands and thousands of innocent babies continue to be slaughtered each month.

God is not happy with *any nation* that says unborn babies are disposable and can be thrown into wastepaper bins at the whim of a judge, a doctor, a legislature, or an unwilling parent. The Lion is roaring over our treatment of women and our exploitation of children and the unborn. Once, twice, God's mercy, God's grace. Three times, God's grace and mercy is extended for yet another chance. Then the line is crossed, and the Lion roars. At that point, unavoidable judgment is about to descend upon a nation.

The Lion roars when we have no respect for the elderly, the dying, and the dead. God declared through Amos, "...For three sins of Moab, even for four, I will not turn back My wrath. Because he burned, as if to lime, the bones of Edom's king" (Amos 2:1). God is saying, "These are My children who are made in My image. My judgment will fall upon every nation that mistreats the elderly and the dying, and abuses the bodies of the dead." God notices when individuals, nations, and even churches treat people like things or objects. The Lion has roared.

2. The Lion roars when we break commitments, covenants, and treaties.

"...For three sins of Tyre, even for four, I will not turn back My wrath. Because she sold whole communities of captives to Edom, *disregarding a treaty* of brotherhood" (Amos 1:9). If a nation makes an agreement with another nation and then breaks the agreement or covenant, that first nation risks earning God's judgment. He takes it very seriously when individuals or nations publicly commit to a popular cause or a key action, but behind the scenes follow the path of wickedness and break a spoken commitment, treaty, or agreement. God demands that we keep and honor every treaty of brotherhood.

I expected to see God judging idolatry, but in the Book of Amos, He was judging a nation for breaking a treaty of brotherhood. I thought, *Lord, we need a new perspective on what it means to walk together in families. We need to have a new perspective in church, to understand that every time we open our mouths and speak critically about a brother or a sister, You are unhappy with our actions.* God commands a blessing where people dwell together in unity, but He roars when we break commitments and stray into disunity, when we speak against other churches, leaders, or individuals, and act like divorce is "just a thing that happens."

The Lion is roaring loudly today, but we are still in a day of grace when God is working with us to make our hearts clean. He wants our hearts to beat with His heart of love for people. God loves unborn children. God loves the elderly and those facing death in our hospitals today. God wants the Church to rise up and begin to speak on their behalf against injustice, and to declare the good news of Jesus.

When God turns His attention on Judah and Israel in the Book of Amos, He talks about the commitments those nations made to God and then violated. "...For three sins of Judah [people of God], even for four, I will not turn back My wrath. Because they have rejected the law of the Lord and have not kept His decrees, because they have been led astray by false gods, the gods their ancestors followed. I will send fire upon Judah that will consume the fortresses of Jerusalem" (Amos 2:4-5). The judgment of God will follow broken relationships and broken covenants.

I began to ask myself how many times I'd promised the Lord, "I'll follow You, Lord Jesus, whatever the cost. I want to please You." Yet I would find myself doing what I ought not do at times. We all need to understand that our "yes" must mean yes, and our "no" must mean no. That goes for our commitments to other people as well. God wants to fill us with a clear sense of the reality of the consequences when we fail to keep our commitments. How many people have we let down? How many covenants have we broken? How many treaties has our nation broken?

We need to examine our hearts. We need to catch something of God's heart so He can take us on to the next phase of His move in the earth. God isn't interested in just refreshing the Church for some good times. He has sent His refreshing for a divine purpose. We are being refreshed, we are receiving a new zeal and sense of purpose, so we can accomplish His purposes in the "real world." It's time to prophetically *roar* at injustices that grieve the heart of God.

3. The Lion roars when we exploit the poor and the underprivileged.

This is what the Lord says: "For three sins of Israel, even for four, I will not turn back My wrath. They sell the righteous for silver, and the needy for a pair of sandals. They trample on the heads of the poor as upon the dust of the ground and deny justice to the oppressed. Father and son use the same girl and so profane My holy name. They lie down beside every altar on garments taken in pledge. In the house of their god they drink wine taken as fines" (Amos 2:6-8).

God takes notice when people unjustly abuse people who have fallen down through difficult circumstances. His eye never leaves the plight of the poor. He remembers every act of mistreatment toward women. He sees every individual or nation who exploits the helpless and tramples on the heads of the poor. (I wouldn't want to be in the offender's shoes.)

Is the Lion Roaring at My Nation?

In Amos 5:11, the Lion of Judah roars, "You trample on the poor and force him to give you grain. Therefore, though you have built stone mansions, you will not live in them; though you have planted lush vineyards, you will not drink their wine." The Lion is roaring in anger today. God takes seriously the way the poor and the underprivileged of our world are treated. The anger of God is growing stronger with every passing day. As I made my way through the Book of Amos, I began to wonder, *What if Britain's name were inserted in these sentences of judgment? If the verse read, "This is what the Lord says, for three sins of Britain, even for four, I will not turn back My wrath…" would it fit?* I wondered if God is forming another declaration today that thunders, "This is what the Lord says, for three sins of the United States, even for four, I will not turn back My wrath…."

I am afraid that we find it all too easy to treat people as things today. We live in an "abortion generation" where thousands of innocent lives are snuffed out in unspeakable violence every day without an ounce of emotion or guilt. A broadening river of pornography and explicit sexual exploitation videos are flooding into virtually every nation on earth, much of it produced and distributed by the United States, Canada, and Great Britain. It is a simple thing to acquire and even sell illegal drugs in most major cities across the world, and everywhere we see the cruel exploitation of the poor continuing.

Even the Church stands guilty of treating people as commodities or disposable items that can be discarded and replaced once they've "done their thing" (as if these people aren't needed anymore). History and the daily news confirm that virtually every nation on earth has flagrantly broken commitments and treaties. And the Lion is roaring.

My purpose here is not to condemn but to say this: *Were it not for grace and God's extended love and mercy, I believe we would stand on the brink of the judgments of God.* Fortunately, Amos doesn't leave us teetering on the brink of judgment. His message also reveals the compassionate heart of God who is full of mercy. Dr. Philip Hickerton, one of the staff pastors at New Life Fellowship here in Britian, gave a word of prophecy that perfectly describes God's heart for us today: "God is far more interested in forgiveness than condemnation."

It's Time for the Church to Roar!

We are living in a very exciting time. Yes, the Lion is roaring in our generation, but He is blessing His Church to show us His heart. He is blessing us so that we can *be* a blessing. He has called and empowered us to be a prophetic Church that will roar and speak out about injustices. God is angry over injustice, and He wants to birth something in this nation through His Church. He wants to birth a great revival with power that will turn the nations around and address the issues of abortion, hatred, loneliness, and fear. Make no mistake, there has always been a godly link between revival and social action! When God breathes on the Church, the Church responds by working and serving in His name.

We need to carry the very heart of God into intercession and prayer so our nations will be forgiven and cleansed. Amos looked to a new day of deliverance. God's grace is being extended today, and we are seeing more people becoming Christians than ever before on the face of the earth! Perhaps Amos was seeing a day like today as he pronounced a prophecy over Israel that also applies to the whole earth in Christ:

> *"The days are coming," declares the Lord, "when the reaper will be overtaken by the plowman and the planter by the one treading grapes. New wine will drip from the mountains and flow from all the hills. I will bring back My exiled people Israel; they will rebuild the ruined cities and live in them. They will plant vineyards and drink their wine; they will make gardens and eat their fruit"* (Amos 9:13-14).

Chapter 5

Awakening the Oil-Filled Church

*Then the angel who talked with me returned and **wakened** me, **as a man is wakened from his sleep**. He asked me, "What do you see?"... (Zechariah 4:1-2).*

A sleeping giant is sprawled across every continent and island nation of the earth. The potential of beauty is in her face and form, but her overlong slumber has dimmed her beauty and silenced her voice. Her garments have been soiled through decades of slumber during which her bed of repose has become unclean and unwholesome. The sleeper's true strength, power, and identity are unknown in our age. Yet there is One who has come to awaken His sleeping love, to urge her to adorn herself with beauty and holiness as a bride preparing for a wedding feast.

Zechariah the prophet could be called the prophet of renewal and revival because his prophecy contains the program of God for the awakening and resurrection of His victorious Church and Bride. The goal of God's plan is to awaken an *oil-filled* Church so it can bring light to the whole world with its godly fire.

> *He asked me, "What do you see?" I answered, "I see a solid gold lampstand with a bowl at the top and seven lights on it, with seven channels to the lights. Also there are two olive trees by it, one on the right of the bowl and the other on its left." I asked the angel who talked with me, "What are these, my lord?"* (Zechariah 4:2-4)

Once the prophet of God asks the question, "What are these, my lord?" he receives an answer that speaks directly to any age or generation blessed with God's special visitation in the work of revival.

> *He answered, "Do you not know what these are?" "No, my lord," I replied. So he said to me, "This is the word of the Lord to Zerubbabel: 'Not by might nor by power, but by My Spirit,' says the Lord Almighty. What are you, O mighty mountain? Before Zerubbabel you will become level ground. Then he will bring out the capstone to shouts of 'God bless it! God bless it!' " Then the word of the Lord came to me: "The hands of Zerubbabel have laid the foundation of this temple; his hands will also complete it. Then you will know that the Lord Almighty has sent me to you. Who despises the day of small things? Men will rejoice when they see the plumb line in the hand of Zerubbabel. (These seven are the eyes of the Lord, which range throughout the earth.)" Then I asked the angel, "What are these two olive trees on the right and the left of the lampstand?" Again I asked him, "What are these two olive branches beside the two gold pipes that pour out golden oil?" He replied, "Do you not know what these are?" "No, my lord," I said. So he said, "These are the two who are **anointed to serve the Lord** of all the earth"* (Zechariah 4:5-14).

Zerubbabel, the prince of Judah, is a historic character chosen to play a key role in God's temple rebuilding program. He is mentioned by name in Zechariah's prophecy along with Joshua, the high priest of the day. In Zechariah chapter 3, Joshua had a renewal experience. His sins were washed away and he was cleansed so he could be used by God in this rebuilding program.

One thing we should notice is that the Israelites started the rebuilding process by building an *altar* first. They started with worship, and then they moved outward from the Presence of God to rebuild the temple and the walls of Jerusalem. These builders faced a lot of obstacles and persecution along the way, but the temple was built and the walls restored. So these prophecies were delivered in advance of and in the midst of great revival! We also need to understand that the idea of separating "the sacred" from "the secular" is a relatively new idea (and one that didn't come from God). All the Israelites knew, and all the first-century believers knew, that you just followed God or you didn't. You gave Him your whole life or nothing. It was unthinkable that a Christian would reserve part of his or her life as a "God-free zone."

Even in the Old Testament, God blessed Israel so that Israel could be a blessing. He brought renewal and revival to Israel so He could ultimately bring the Messiah through that nation to bless the entire world. He has never been interested in revamping the Church for its own sake, which is equal to "rearranging the deck chairs on the Titanic." The Church is not a sinking ship; it is a Heaven-sent lifeboat for the perishing, a vessel of blessing for those in need. That calling and anointing only intensifies to a fever pitch when God brings revival to the land. The problem is that we (the members of the Church) are not very good at going into all the world.

We need to be awakened to the passion of the Lord, and my task is to motivate you and my other friends in the Church to become the oil-filled Church of God's desire. Zechariah motivated the people of Israel to restore the gates and the walls that had been destroyed. Then as now, the Word of the Lord comes to us: " 'Not by might nor by power, but by My Spirit,' says the Lord Almighty" (Zech. 4:6b).

We all recognize the awesome move of God on the earth today. Now we need to face the facts: You and I just aren't adequate to the task. We need God's power and strength. We need His Word to light our way and His Spirit to set us on fire as we speak with neighbors, friends, and other people in our ordinary lives. I am reminded of John Wesley's inspired answer to a question about how he drew crowds: "I set myself on fire, and the people come to see me burn."

Revival is the fruit of hunger and obedience in the Church (not just the clergy). I feel more called than ever before to equip the saints for the work of the ministry. Who are the saints? You are.

During my study of the Book of Zechariah, the Spirit of God revealed to me that God wants to awaken the Church to some things that are vital to His purposes in our day. I will give you three of them in this chapter.

Awakened to See

*Then the angel who talked with me returned and **wakened** me, as a man is wakened from his sleep. He asked me, "**What do you see?**..."* (Zechariah 4:1-2).

God is arousing His Church to ask the question, "What do you see?" Most Bible commentators say Zechariah wasn't actually asleep. He was simply so involved in "life as usual" that he just wasn't "seeing." Are you so involved in your normal routine (or "religious" rut) that you are blind to what God is doing right in front of your nose? A powerful prophecy was delivered to our local church one week before I delivered this message on "awakening the oil-filled Church" to our local fellowship. The prophecy said, "Nobody really sees or hears about the earthquake—it's just the instruments that pick it up." God is awakening His early-warning system, the prophets. They need to be awakened to see. I want to be awake to see.

Frankly, we need God's help just to see His arrival in our neighborhood most of the time. Elijah's servant had trouble seeing the provision of God until he had obeyed the prophet and looked for the seventh time! Only then did he return to his master and say what he saw: "A cloud as small as a man's hand is rising from the sea" (1 Kings 18:44a).

When God awakens us, we begin to see something. I believe that our eyes have been opened to see fields that are white to harvest and ready for the picking. Our eyes are finally open to see a change taking place across the globe. We must *see* it before God can show us what He wants us to do about it. Once we see it with His eyes, He can ignite our passion for the lost.

Just what did Zechariah see, and does it apply to our situation today? Since the answer to the second part of the question is a resounding "yes," then we need to closely examine what Zechariah saw.

Zechariah saw a golden lampstand topped by a bowl or receptacle used to hold oil. He also saw an olive tree on either side of the lampstand. (The Hebrew word for olive, *zayith*, comes from a root word meaning "to be prominent; or brightness,"[1] from the common use of pure olive oil as a fuel for lamps.) Two channels or tubes lead from the oil-filled bowl to the seven lamps at the top of the golden lampstand. Many of the oldest and most respected Bible commentators think there were seven of these channels or tubes for each lamp, meaning there were 49 channels of fresh oil to the lamps of God's Presence. Could this be a picture of Jubilee? (See Leviticus 25:8.)

Envision this lampstand in your mind for a moment. Do you see something now? Like Zechariah before you, if you apply this to God's Kingdom, you will begin to see that when God's people start to do things by the anointing of His Spirit instead of by human understanding, then their light will shine into the darkness! Their power Source is living and inexhaustible. Although they were once ostracized, belittled, and cursed as Jerusalem was, they, too, will shine again with the illumination of God glory! God's purposes will be fulfilled in the earth as His prophetic light is lit up again.

I believe that Zechariah's prophecy, like so many others in the Old Testament, was a dual prophecy. It not only applied literally to the historical context of his day, but it also applied to the great harvest to take place beyond his day on the other side of the cross. In fact, Zechariah's prophecy is full of Messianic promises about the One who was destined to become the Light of the world. He predicts the unlimited supply of the olive oil, signifying the abundant flow of the Holy Spirit without measure. If you follow this symbolism through right into the New Testament, you will find that Zechariah was really seeing *an oil-filled Church*!

The golden lampstand has been a symbol throughout the Scriptures of God's people shining into the darkness. This imagery is picked up in the New Testament and culminates in the Book of Revelation, where seven local churches are seen as lampstands commissioned to light up the darkness. Zechariah was awakened to see an *oil-filled Church*. You and I need to ask God to awaken us and show us the same thing.

The respected Bible commentator, Matthew Henry, wrote about this oil flowing from the olive trees through the channels to the lampstands more than 200 years ago. He said, "Without any further care, they received oil as fast as they wasted it. They never wanted, nor were ever glutted, and so kept always burning clear."[2] I love that line. Matthew Henry saw an unglutted Church, a Church where there was a freedom for the Holy Spirit to move in its every channel. That is what God wants us to see in our generation. This is more than an academic subject—this is on the verge of being a genuine reality. But first we must be awakened to *see* the will of God for the Church.

Right now we're familiar with "glutted church life" where even the best things go stale. We're used to living in the static church of yesterday, not the dynamic church of the now. One of the most important things for us to see about this oil-filled Church is its ultimate purpose: *God lights our lamps so we can light up the darkness with His glory!*

What would happen in the Church if man stepped out of the way so the Holy Spirit could really be let loose? What would happen if the Holy Spirit's fresh oil was poured through our young people, through our children's work, through our older people, and through our evangelistic opportunities? I believe we need to be awakened to see God's great Church fulfilling His will with an unlimited supply of anointing and Holy Ghost power!

We need to see more than the staggering darkness, degradation, brokenness, loneliness, and fear in our world. God wants us to catch a vision of an *oil-filled Church* (no, not the so-called superministries and big names) composed of ordinary people filled with the extraordinary power of fresh oil pouring through them! Would the world ever be the same?

This is what I'm living for at the moment. This is what the Church is all about. It's about fresh oil being poured through all the channels, mechanisms, and relationships of God's family on earth, the Church. If God gets His hands upon all of us— if He can get His hands upon us as a corporate people and plant vision in us—what can be accomplished in this generation? Where will we be after five or ten years of total obedience and submission to Jesus Christ?

Awakened to Speak

In Zechariah's vision, we also witness the angel of the Lord saying to a people who have had no voice, "These are the things you are to do: Speak the truth to each other" (Zech. 8:16a). In the outpouring of the Spirit, there will always be the emergence of the prophetic, and we need to release it. Prophets play a key role in the work of restoration and revival. "Then Zerubbabel son of Shealtiel and Jeshua son of Jozadak set to work to rebuild the house of God in

Jerusalem. And the prophets of God were with them, helping them" (Ezra 5:2). The best prophetic ministry always comes behind the builders in the oil-filled Church.

When Zechariah admitted that he didn't understand what he had seen, the angel of God basically said, beginning in Zechariah 4:6, "Look, Zerubbabel is going to have to do this thing. Now I know that at the moment, nothing is being built. There aren't even any foundations for the temple, but the Word is out; and prophetically that word needs supporting: It's not by might or power; it's by My Spirit, says the Lord" (my paraphrase of Zechariah 4:6).

Too many times we get hung up on the word, *might* in this great promise. This word in the Hebrew, *chayil*, can refer variously to "a force, whether of men, means or other resources; an army, wealth, virtue, valor, or strength."[3] The Church is not going to grow by man's wealth, influence, or reputation, and it's not going to grow by man's power either.

Too often, church leaders do whatever they *think* is right, only to find themselves stretched to the limit and unable to do anything more. Then they wonder why the breakthrough still doesn't come. What has happened? They've forgotten God's revelation to Zechariah: It's not by might; it's not by power; it's not by wealth, influence, or reputation; it's not even by stretching yourself and your people to the limit in Christ's name. God's will is done when the power of the Holy Spirit does through us what we could not stretch far enough to do on our own.

God does amazing things in amazing ways when we line up behind Him in obedience. He raised up a pagan Persian king named Cyrus and used his earthly authority and resources to help Zerubbabel and Jeshua (Joshua) rebuild the temple of the Jews and the walls of Jerusalem. Only God could make something that inconceivable come to pass. In our day, we should never forget that God is as much at work in the world as He is in the Church, and the two are going to come together through His redemptive work.

The angel also gave prophetic instructions concerning what should be said and done when God does His work: "What are you, O mighty mountain? Before Zerubbabel you will become level ground. Then he will bring out the capstone to shouts of 'God bless it! God bless it!' " (Zech. 4:7) This prophetic word is saying to Zerubbabel, "It's going to happen. The foundations *will* be rebuilt, so keep on going! God will give you the strength."

How many times have you felt like poor Zerubbabel, a man who was expected to tackle an impossible task armed only with a plumb line in his hand? I know that in my life, God has somehow reassured me just as He spoke through His messenger to Zechariah: "Who despises the day of small things? Men will rejoice when they see the plumb line in the hand of Zerubbabel" (Zech. 4:10a). God's prophetic voice said, "Hang on a minute, if you have your eyes open. The people will rejoice when they see this man I've chosen holding up a plumb line. Why? Because they will believe that ultimately My purposes and plans *are* going to come to pass."

You may be speaking into situations that you are beginning to see, and wondering if you're right or terribly wrong. I tell you that if God has given you a mandate and placed a plumb line in your hands, then start rejoicing *right now* because God's building program is moving on to completion. Remember that what you *see* and what you *speak* into will make a great deal of difference. It is time to release the prophetic voices among us to speak out the secrets in the heart of God for this generation and His Church. We need to heed the wise counsel of one Bible commentator who said, "Don't look at the apparent feebleness of the church in it's external resources, and overlook it's true glory."[4]

The Answer to a Sin-Filled World

Zechariah was literally seeing God's divine answer to a sin-filled world—*the oil-filled Church*. God invaded our world in the form of His Son, Jesus Christ, the *anointed* one. What does that mean? Jesus was the Messiah (*Mashiyach* in Hebrew) and Christ (*Christos* in Greek), which means in both languages, "anointed one." The Son of God was touched with the holy oil of consecration. He was covered by and filled with the Holy Spirit and all the power that comes through the Spirit. What He declared about Himself, He was also declaring over His Church, which was destined to be birthed through His obedience on the cross. He opened the scroll of Isaiah in the sabbath in His thirtieth year and He said, "The Spirit of the Lord is on Me, because He has anointed Me..." (Lk. 4:18). "He has *Christed* Me, He has *Mashiyached* Me with oil."

God is opening our eyes today to *see* a vision of the Body of Christ touched with that same anointing. Can you see it? The same oil anointing that was upon Jesus is dripping onto the Church right now. The same things that Jesus did under and through that anointing are beginning to happen in and through His people! The oil-filled Church exhibits oil-filled finances, oil-filled evangelism, oil-filled and Holy Spirit-touched singing, preaching, and healing! Can you see this oil-filled Church beginning to shine through the darkness in our generation?

If you have eyes to see and ears to hear the things that God is doing in the earth today, then you are in for some very exciting and unusual experiences! There's an oil-filled youth culture emerging from the Church that is seeing, saying, and doing things that I wish I'd experienced when I was younger! God is raising up a "revival culture" in every demographic group that is breaking through age-old barriers to invade every man's darkness!

I believe God is raising up a generation of oil-filled believers who will dare to declare God's prophetic word to the world as well as to the Church. They will boldly inject and declare God's prophetic words of truth into controversial issues of injustice. Prisoners will be set free and captives will be released from prisons as the oil-filled Church, the redeemer Church, taps the unlimited power of God in Jesus' name and anointing.

An oil-filled Church cannot help but ultimately impact society. *It has to happen.* Light cannot hide in a dark place. We will no longer be content just to have "good meetings." The oil-filled Church will have good meetings *and* make a powerful and lasting impact on the world around it. The oil-filled Church *always makes a difference*! God is out to awaken His oil-filled Church. He wants to awaken us to see, to hear, and to serve!

Awakened to Serve

When Zechariah saw the great vision of the golden lampstand with the seven lamps and the oil flowing through 49 channels, he understood a lot of it. He knew what the angel meant when he said, " 'Not by might nor by power, but by My Spirit,' says the Lord Almighty" (Zech. 4:6b). He knew the oil stood for God's flowing anointing.

But toward the end of Zechariah 4, the prophet basically said, "Angel, I do have one little question…What are these two trees on either side, because if I can understand where the flow comes from, then possibly we can make a difference" (see Zech. 4:12). The angel answered, "These are the two who are *anointed* to serve the Lord of all the earth" (Zech. 4:14). The Amplified Bible puts it this way: "…These are the two *sons of oil* [Joshua the high priest and Zerubbabel the prince of Judah, the two anointed ones] who stand before the Lord of the whole earth [as His anointed instruments]" (Zech. 4:14 AMP).

I believe that the angel was explaining to Zechariah that the two olive trees in the vision were feeding life into the mechanisms of what God was doing. Zerubbabel and Joshua were just two ordinary men picked and chosen by God to re-build the temple against all odds. He anointed them to be-come trees that were continually being filled with fresh oil that would bless and inspire Israel to do the work of rebuilding. History tells us that the temple was rebuilt and the walls of Je-rusalem actually restored because the people were motivated.

How did this "impossible" job got done? God took hold of ordinary people and filled them with His extraordinary oil of supernatural anointing! Then He basically said, "Now that I've filled you, you are anointed to *get on with the business.* Now fill the Church with ministry and life in the power of the Spirit. Do what I've anointed you to do, and as you do it, there will be *more* fresh oil."

The Hebrew word for fresh oil is *yitshar.* As God's fresh oil of anointing is poured through the mechanisms of church life, things will begin to change forever. Now what is the ulti-mate destination and purpose of this oil according to Zechariah's vision? The two trees? No. The collection bowl? No. The tubes leading to the seven lights? No. All of these are carriers and transporters of God's anointing. The ultimate destiny and purpose for God's oil of anointing on the oil-filled Church is to *light up the darkness with God's glory!* When God's oil of anointing flows through the oil-filled Church, every instrument in the "mechanism" of the Church is touched and covered by the oil. But the chief fruit and work of the lampstand is to produce light to pierce the darkness around it!

So when we talk about revival, keep this vision of the oil-filled Church in your mind. Yes, the Lord will use a few anointed trees planted by living waters to ooze an extra abun-dance of the life of God from their lives for the blessing of the Church. But these few anointed trees are only a part of God's lampstand! I pray that God will raise up every member of the Body of Christ today to be oil-filled, Holy Spirit-anointed and baptized instruments of light to shine the glory of Jesus Christ into the darkness over our cities, regions, and nations. The only way God's vision will come to pass is if you and I get filled with fresh oil and allow our mouths to be loosed to speak out as bold witnesses to the glory of Christ Jesus. God is awakening us to serve the Lord of all the earth. Jesus was direct and to the point:

> *Ye are the **light of the world**. A city that is set on an hill cannot be hid. Neither do men light a candle, and put it under a bushel, but on a candlestick; and it giveth light unto all that are in the house. Let your light so shine before men, that they may see your good works, and glorify your Father which is in heaven* (Matthew 5:14-16 KJV).

God has anointed His Church to see the vision, to speak the vision, and to serve and carry out the vision. It is time for the oil-filled Church to rise up as fiery lamps filled with His brilliant glory to boldly shine into the dark world! We are anointed to serve and to shine with His anointing oil into the darkness of the lost.

Everything in Zechariah's vision speaks of Jesus Christ. In Zerubbabel we have the kingly ministry. In Joshua (or more correctly, *Jehoshua*, or Jesus) we have the priestly ministry. In Zechariah we have the prophetic ministry. This is a beautiful picture of our Lord Jesus, the anointed prophet, priest, and King of kings. We have a responsibility to respond to this vision because it is a *rhema* word, a living word to every member of Christ's Body today. Pray this prayer with me right where you are:

> *"Holy Spirit, will You awaken us corporately? Awake O Zion! Wake up, O sleeper! Wake us up to what You are doing, Lord. Make us obedient servants. Touch us now and anoint our eyes with **yitshar**, Your fresh oil, that we may see. Touch our lips with holy fire from Your altar that we may speak. Release us to serve the Lord of all the earth and make us wise in Your ways.*

> *"O God, there is a gospel-shaped vacuum emerging in people around the world. Lord, we ask that You will anoint Your people to speak to the captives with prophetic boldness. Anoint us to prophetically speak Your life into our places of employment, into our schools. Anoint us to take our stand for justice and for Your will in the earth. Anoint our heads with oil and empower us to help the helpless in Jesus' name and authority.*
>
> *"Bind us together as one Body even as You are anointing these prophetic ministries into their places of work, worship, and service. May You receive all of the glory, in Jesus' name."*

Now whatever God tells you to do, *do it!* The coming revival will only succeed and fulfill God's purposes if everyone does what God has called he or she to do.

Endnotes

1. *Strong's*, **olive** (Hebrew, #2122, 2099).

2. *Matthew Henry's Commentary*, on the olive trees and golden lampstand described in Zechariah 4:1-3,11-14.

3. *Strong's*, **might** (Hebrew, #2428).

4. T.V. Moore, *The Geneva Series of Commentaries* (Edinburgh, Scotland: The Banner of Truth Trust), p. 80.

Chapter 6

Rediscover the Power of Blessing

After what many people would describe as a long drought and season of difficulty for the Church, I am happy to report that God is thoroughly blessing His Church today. His blessing isn't coming in a trickle or a smooth flow though. It is flooding through our ranks in overflowing, abundant waves of favor, anointing, strength, and overwhelming love. It is a force that is moving and transforming the Church itself into an instrument of blessing day by day. If you are wondering what in the world I am talking about, then you are going to positively love this chapter!

We need to understand what a "blessing" is if we are going to understand the things God is saying to us about it today. According to *Webster's Collegiate Dictionary*, a *blessing* is "the act or words of one that blesses, approval, encouragement; and a thing conducive to happiness or welfare."[1] The verb, *to bless*, means variously "to hallow or consecrate by religious rite or word, to invoke divine care for; to praise, glorify, to speak well of or approve; to confer prosperity or happiness upon; to endow or favor."[2]

Blessed So We Can Bless

I believe that we—individually and together as the Church of Jesus Christ—are blessed so we can bless. Now over the last few years, the Church world has heard all kinds of things about blessing.

When God's Presence descended upon Toronto Airport Vineyard Fellowship (now Toronto Airport Christian Fellowship), many people were rather disturbed when the phenomenon came to be called "the Toronto Blessing." (I thought it odd that no one raised a ruckus over what theologians and historians alike call "the Welsh revivals." I suppose no one protested at the time because it seemed logical since the revivals occurred in Wales. I personally am thankful to God for all that He has been doing through Toronto, regardless of what title is attached to "the blessing.")

We tend to use the word, *blessing*, in a flippant manner much of the time. If somebody sneezes, we automatically say in a thoughtless monotone, "God bless you." The truth is that the blessing of God is a very wonderful thing. Wherever you find God's blessing, you find happy and prosperous people who enjoy all the benefits of God's favor.

I believe that God wants His people to be happy, but I didn't always think this way. Like countless numbers of Christians around the world, I was brought up in a belief system where we thought (and were taught) that we weren't *really* meant to be happy. In fact, if you were happy, then it was almost certain that you were rather naughty! We were told that it wasn't happiness that was required, but joy. That "joy," of course, had to be fairly deep, or it would lead to the unhappy conclusion that you were happy (which again indicated that you were probably rather naughty).

The happiness of God's people has less to do with the changing circumstances of life than with the happiness experienced while surrounded by God's unfailing love and favor. Even in a natural family with healthy relationships, children seem "happier" when Dad is home than when he is out of town on a business trip. They may still have a difficult time on certain days, but overall they are just happier. God's people just tend to be happier most of the time because "Dad" is forever home and doting on His children. Our general state of happiness should be an unavoidable by-product of God's continual favor in our lives.

Christians are not automatically exempt from problems and difficulties. Indeed, the Scriptures tell us, "In fact, everyone who wants to live a godly life in Christ Jesus will be persecuted" (2 Tim. 3:12). Every Christian will have issues to face and painful trials to endure. We will not always be laughing, but we know we will never have to live a single day outside of God's canopy of love. We have an "edge" in our human struggles because we know that underneath and round about us are the everlasting arms of God, and before and behind us is God's favor.

What do the Scriptures and the original biblical languages have to say about blessing? Solomon wrote of the bride in the Songs, "The maidens saw her and called her blessed…" (Song 6:9b). That means the maidens "declared her happy." The Bible says in Genesis 1:22, "God *blessed* them and said, 'Be fruitful and increase in number….'" In the first Psalm, the literal translation of the very first word, *'esher*, is "how happy!"[3] "Blessed—*how happy!*—is the man…" (Ps. 1:1a).

An interesting word turns up in the New Testament in the Gospel of Matthew where Jesus said, "But I say unto you, Love your enemies, *bless* them that curse you, do good to them that hate you, and pray for them which despitefully use you, and persecute you" (Mt. 5:44 KJV). The Greek word translated as "bless" is *eulogeo*, which is similar to our English word, *eulogize*. It literally means "to speak well of." Although the natural man may find it easier to pull people down with our words, God wants us to be instruments of His blessing.

The beatitudes in the Gospel of Matthew offer us a powerful series of blessings invoked by the Son of God. Every time you see the word *blessed* in this anointed sermon, you can accurately translate it as "happy." God is declaring His blessing and favor over the Church today. Although many people think that God is out to get us or punish us in some way, the Scriptures are very clear: God intends to bless His people and overshadow them with His glorious Presence.

A rather obscure passage in God's Word beautifully describes the blessing our Father is declaring over the Church today. Like so many prophetic passages from the Old Testament, it applies to the Church just as it applied to Israel in Zephaniah's day:

> *Sing, O Daughter of Zion; shout aloud, O Israel! Be glad and rejoice with all your heart, O Daughter of Jerusalem! The Lord has taken away your punishment, He has turned back your enemy. The Lord, the King of Israel, is with you; never again will you fear any harm. On that day they will say to Jerusalem, "Do not fear, O Zion; do not let your hands hang limp. The Lord your God is with you, He is mighty to save. He will take great delight in you, He will quiet you with His love, He will rejoice over you with singing"* (Zephaniah 3:14-17).

This is how the blessing of God is expressed to His people. The first thing I want you to notice is that He has called us to rejoice and be happy again. The second thing is that the Lord has taken away our punishment (even though we deserved it). If that's not blessing, then I don't know what is. Thirdly, the Lord has turned back the enemy. God is declaring His blessing over a people who have been brought out of Egypt as it were, and brought into the promised land (which is His Presence). When God arrived, the enemy of our souls lost all rights of dominion over us. Our freedom was won that day Jesus Christ, the Son of God, rose from the dead. He is alive, and He is the victorious King.

I thank God that He has chosen *not* to be a remote God hiding in Heaven. In Zephaniah 3:17, God Himself promised us intimacy. The King of Israel, Immanuel, is *with us*. God has declared this blessing over us as His Church: "He will take great delight in you, He will quiet you with His love, He will rejoice over you with singing" (Zeph. 3:17b). God has pushed the enemy back, but more than that, He wants an intimate relationship with us! According to the New Testament, the God of Heaven has become our Father and now we can cry, "Abba, Daddy Father!" (see Rom. 8:14-17; Gal. 4:6-7) God is saying to us today, "I want to bless you, My children. I am your heavenly Father."

From the start of the Old Testament to the end of the New Testament, God has packed His Word with blessings! God wants His people to be blessed.

This is the great revelation of the New Testament: God our heavenly Father wants to bless us. He wants to fill us with a sense of intimacy expressed in the Song of Solomon, "My beloved is mine, and I am his..." (Song 2:16 KJV). Jesus wants to *eulogize* or speak well over His Church.

God has also blessed us with new strength. "...Do not fear, O Zion; do not let your hands hang limp. The Lord your God is with you, He is mighty to save" (Zeph. 3:16-17a). God wants His people to be strong. Many churches today feel helpless in a rampaging world, and their witness is as useless as a soldier with his hands hanging limp in passivity and defeat. God has pronounced His blessing over the Church to bring us strength! Not only that, but God also tells us that He has brought us salvation—from sin, from hell, and from destruction. This is the blessing of God upon His people.

God's final blessing just seems out of place in many of our stuffy religious institutions and rigid agendas. God literally declares through the prophet, "He will quiet you with His love, He will rejoice over you with singing" (Zeph. 3:17b). Now there's a concept. Can you imagine the scene in the spirit realm when God begins to dance over His people? (That's no place for devils to be.) The Book of Revelation records specific things that Jesus Christ spoke to specific churches. I wonder if God has specific songs for specific churches? All I know is that there is *a singing God* who loves to sing blessings, victory, deliverance, and freedom over the Church of Jesus Christ, whether it is to a small group of two or more gathered in Jesus' name, or a vibrant congregation of 6,000 or more gathered in a praise celebration.

Capture and hold fast to this revelation of the Lord: God Almighty is singing over you this very moment! He delights in *eulogizing* over you each day! F.B. Meyer has said, "He will rejoice over the soul that finds its all in Himself." Jesus is the center of all this. As we yield to Him and make Jesus the center of our lives, then I believe that the blessing of God can fall upon us individually and as a people united under His name.

It Is Time for You to Bless!

The second aspect of "blessing" in God's plan concerns *our* responsibility as adopted sons and daughters to personally declare blessings over the Church, its leaders, and one another.

We already know about our natural tendency—even as Christians—to be negative rather than positive. God wants you and I to change our thinking about pronouncing blessings over other people. We need to change our language to become encouragers rather than discouragers! We need to become prophetic people who continually build up, strengthen, and edify others. Too many people try to use prophecy for the opposite reasons. When we hear these people say, "I've got a word from the Lord for you..." we automatically think, *Well, I'd better put on my safety helmet—it's bound to be something bad.*

Men and women have always played a role in the task of blessing. The God-ordained function of pronouncing blessings is found throughout the Bible, but there are two major kinds of blessings that are especially important to the Church today: the "Aaronic blessing" of the Old Testament and the "apostolic blessing" of the New Testament.

In the Old Testament, the Aaronic priests were specifically told to bless the people of God. Under the New Covenant of grace, we have all been made kings and priests unto our God. That means it is the task of *every believer* to pronounce blessing.

The Aaronic Blessing

The Lord said to Moses, "Tell Aaron and his sons, 'This is how you are to bless the Israelites. Say to them: "The Lord bless you and keep you; the Lord make His face shine upon you and be gracious to you; the Lord turn His face toward you and give you peace." ' So they will put My name on the Israelites, and I will bless them" (Numbers 6:22-27).

Isn't this fascinating? God gave Moses a framework with very specific guidelines for blessing the people of God. He said, "Tell Aaron and his sons that if they want to bless Israel, then this is how they should do it. This is what they say...." Then God gave them one of the oldest and most beautiful poetry prayers in Scripture. We don't get the full meaning of God's heart of blessing in our English translations of the original Hebrew.

First of all, notice how the name of the Lord is the central focus of every line. "The *Lord* bless you and keep you; the *Lord* make His face shine upon you and be gracious to you; the *Lord* turn His face toward you and give you peace." When we bless a people, we need to fill that blessing thoroughly with the Lord! It is the Lord who blesses.

When the blessing says, "The Lord make His face to shine upon you," it gives us a picture of the benevolent look of God's face, of the smiling face of God showing peace and happiness on His people. When the blessing says that God will be "gracious" to us, it means He will "bend or stoop down in kindness" to us to "bestow His favor."[4] The King James Version says, "The Lord lift up His countenance upon thee" (Num. 6:26a). The phrase "lift up" simply means that God *pays attention* to you.

This Aaronic or priestly blessing in the Old Testament was rooted in the nation, the soil promised by God, in the very substance of who the people were originally blessed to be a blessing to all nations. This blessing would include well-being, good health, prosperity, and salvation through obedience to the Law. God Himself says in verse 27: " So they will *put My name* on the Israelites, and *I* will bless them."

This is very significant. When the priests did their job and pronounced the blessing over the people, then God Himself would personally bless them. Why? By pronouncing the blessing over God's people, the priests were literally putting God's name on them. This may even be similar to putting a mark or a brand on the people to separate them from others.[5] I also understand that the Hebrew construction of this verse puts a pronounced emphasis on what God Himself would do in response.

God personally blesses things legitimately bearing His name and reputation. I praise God for the blessings that men pronounce over me, but the thing I *really* want is the *blessing of God* that surely follows! What does that mean? It means this: "I the Lord who is your provider will bless the people. I the Lord who is your healer will bless the people. I the Lord who is your banner and covering will bless the people. I the Lord who sanctifies and makes holy will bless the people. I Am Jehovah Shalom, and I the Lord your peace, will bless the people. I Am Jehovah Rophe, and I the Lord your Shepherd, will bless you. I the Lord your righteousness will bless you."

God wants His people to learn how to bless! The job of the priesthood then (and now) was to "put the name of the Lord on the people." Isn't that a great thought? Instead, we may say little powerless prayers at the end of meetings and miss the wealth of this inheritance. I like to do this: "I bless you in the grace of the Lord Jesus Christ, the love of God the Father, and the fellowship of the Holy Spirit." When we pronounce the name of God—Father, Son, and Holy Spirit—over the people, then God—Father, Son, and Holy Spirit—begins to bless the people for His name's sake. Are you convinced?

God wants His New Testament priesthood in Jesus Christ to learn how to bless the people of God too. We need to learn how to put the name of the Lord over people. When we pronounce everything that Jesus can do over their lives, then God moves in.

I want to encourage you that there is more of God's blessing to come. The more we begin to fill our prayer time with focused, biblical, Holy Spirit-directed substance, the more we will be vehicles of God's blessing in the earth. As Kingdom people, we need to learn how to bless so we can give away the things God has so freely given to us. We have been blessed to bless.

The Apostolic Blessing

The New Testament contains examples of what I call the "apostolic blessing," and I have to admit that I only recently stumbled onto the things I'm about to share. I have always been interested in Paul because he was an apostle. I used to think that Paul was really a harsh, no-nonsense, "get out of the way I've got a job to do" kind of guy. I just knew that Paul wasn't really like Barnabas, the "Mister Nice Guy" of the Book of Acts. I decided to study Paul's letters to the churches with a particular curiosity about whether he was a "strategy-minded itinerant church planter" or a genuine "people person."

Paul clearly had a brilliant, strategic mind, and had received the finest intellectual training available in the Jewish culture under Gamaliel. But to my surprise, I discovered that Paul's letters are packed with a passion to see individuals, churches, and leaders thoroughly blessed! Paul puts prayers of blessing in two general areas: his apostolic greetings at the beginning of his letters, and in his "apostolic blessing" that appears variously at the beginning and at the end of his letters. These prayer passages are filled with very *specific* kinds of blessings I hadn't noticed before. The things I learned from Paul about blessing have totally changed my prayer life. As we examine Paul's apostolic blessings in the New Testament, I pray that this will enlarge our *capacity to bless*!

Key Elements of Blessing in Paul's Apostolic *Greetings*

1. Grace and Peace

Nearly every letter that Paul wrote to individuals and churches feature the words *grace* and *peace*. Peace was also pronounced over people in the Aaronic blessing, but peace is at the center or heart of the apostolic blessing. We desperately need the *Shalom* of God, the favor and peace of God's incomparable Presence.

Grace and peace appear 14 times in the New Testament, including Paul's greetings in the Book of Romans, First and Second Corinthians, Galatians, Ephesians, Philippians, Colossians, First and Second Thessalonians, Titus, and Philemon. (In First and Second Timothy, Paul adds "mercy" right in the middle of grace and peace. Who knows, perhaps that tells us a little bit about Timothy.)

2. Constant Remembrance

Paul's prayers of blessing always seemed to display constant remembrance of the people whom God had put in his life and ministry. Again and again, we find the apostle modeling constant remembrance before the brethren, as in the Book of Romans: "...constantly I remember you in my prayers at all times..." (Rom. 1:9-10). "...Remembering you in my prayers. I keep asking..." (Eph. 1:16-17). "I thank my God every time I remember you. In all my prayers for all of you..." (Phil. 1:3).

What does that really mean? Perhaps when Paul sat down to dictate a letter to the church at Philippi, he thought of the day he first met Lydia by the riverside (see Acts 16:14). Or do you think he thought about the Philippian jailer and the way God miraculously delivered the apostle from jail and brought the jailor's entire family to Christ (as described in Acts 16)?

3. Overflowing Thankfulness

Paul's apostolic blessings continually overflow with thankfulness:

> *First, I thank my God through Jesus Christ for all of you* (Rom. 1:8a).
> *I always thank God for you because of His grace...* (1 Cor. 1:4).
> *I have not stopped giving thanks for you* (Eph. 1:16a).
> *I thank my God every time I remember you* (Phil. 1:3).

> *We always thank God, the Father of our Lord Jesus Christ, when we pray for you* (Col. 1:3).
> *We always thank God for all of you* (1 Thess. 1:2a).
> *We ought always to thank God for you...* (2 Thess. 1:3).
> *I thank God, whom I serve...as night and day I constantly remember you...* (2 Tim. 1:3).
> *I always thank my God as I remember you in my prayers* (Philem. 4).

These are the kinds of foundational statements that Paul lays before he actually gets into the substance of the blessing. God wants to transform our lives so we will be more and more like Jesus Christ, and Paul was careful to include three very important and very specific elements in his prayers of blessing. If it were up to us, the epistles would have been filled with generic "shotgun" prayers like, "Lord, bless Mum, bless Dad, and bless the children." Thank God Paul prayed differently and helped transform the Church.

Key Elements of Blessing in Paul's Apostolic *Blessings*

1. Power and Strength

The first thing the apostle Paul prayed for in the lives of his people was that they would receive *power and strength.*

> *He will keep you strong to the end* (1 Cor. 1:8a).
> *And His incomparably great power for us who believe* (Eph. 1:19a).
> *I pray that out of His glorious riches He may strengthen you with power through His Spirit in your inner being* (Eph. 3:16).
> *Being strengthened with all power according to His glorious might* (Col. 1:11a).

2. Enlightenment and Revelation

Paul was determined to see the disciples, converts, and churches under his oversight receive supernatural *enlightenment and revelation.*

> *...May give you the Spirit of wisdom and revelation, so that you may
> know Him better. I pray also that the eyes of your heart may be en-
> lightened...* (Eph. 1:17-18).
>
> *And to know this love that surpasses knowledge* (Eph. 3:19a).
>
> *...That your love may abound more and more in knowledge and depth
> of insight, so that you may be able to discern...* (Phil. 1:9-10).
>
> *...Asking God to fill you with the knowledge of His will through all
> spiritual wisdom and understanding* (Col. 1:9).

3. Love and Witness

The third thing the apostle Paul packs into his pastoral letters is what I call "love and witness." That is receiving God's
love and then walking out that love in terms of our witness to
the world. Paul constantly blessed the people with prayers for
love and witness.

> *...And I pray that you, being rooted and established in love,
> may have power, together with all the saints, to grasp how
> wide and long and high and deep is the love of Christ*
> (Ephesians 3:17-18).
>
> *And this is my prayer: that your love may abound more and
> more...* (Philippians 1:9).
>
> *I pray that you may be active in sharing your faith, so that
> you will have a full understanding of every good thing we
> have in Christ. Your love has given me great joy and encour-
> agement, because you, brother, have refreshed the hearts of
> the saints* (Philemon 6-7).

If you want three prophetic things to pray over people,
pray for power, enlightenment, and love. That will help them
get their eyes opened, so they can go deeper into the things
of God. Why should we pray these things? Because they are
God's desire for His people. The blessing of God isn't limited
to or focused on exterior things. The Creator, our heavenly

Father, is out to get hold of our lives, to transform and change us into His very likeness.

God in Heaven is declaring His blessing over His Church today, but He wants us, as the individual members of His Church, to learn how to declare blessings ourselves. He wants us to bless the Church and the people of God in His name and authority. How? Fill your blessings with Jesus. Fill your blessings with grace, peace, and mercy. Fill your prayers and blessing with constant remembrance of the brethren and with overflowing thankfulness to God for His faithfulness.

We need to give away the things God has given to us. As kings and priests of the Lamb, we need to pray the ancient priestly blessing God gave to Aaron:

The Lord bless you and keep you; the Lord make His face shine upon you and be gracious to you; the Lord turn His face toward you and give you peace (Numbers 6:24-26).

What else should we do? We need to pray that God will give power and strength, with understanding and revelation. We need to ask God to impart His love to His people so it can, in turn, be transformed into a bold and faultless witness that goes out into the world. We need to pray that it goes beyond the church building to spill down the streets of our towns and estates so the blessed people of God *become blessings* everywhere they go. May the people of God become living carriers of the blessing of God.

God doesn't want to see just the Church blessed. He wants the *entire earth* to be blessed and to be filled with His glory. Who is going to do it? Who is going to eulogize over the people of God? Who is going to speak well of people and support them? Who is going to be strong in the Lord? Who is going to be an encourager and a strengthener? I, for one, want to give my life to that. What about you?

If you will permit me, I would like to pronounce the name of the Lord over you in blessing. Although you are reading these words in a book, I believe God will hear and grant my prayer of blessing over your life *just as He honored the apostle Paul's hand-copied letters of blessing* over God's people in the first-century Church.

In the name of Jesus the Lord, I bless you. And may the Lord bless you and keep you—what He has begun in you He is going to finish! May the Lord make His lovely face to shine upon you, and be gracious to you. May the Lord lift up the light of His countenance upon you and turn His face toward you, and may He give you peace.

God promised that if His servants would put His holy name on the people, then He Himself would bless them. Will you receive that blessing right now? Right where you are, you need to receive the blessing of God the Father, God the Son, and God the Holy Spirit over your life. I want to pronounce an apostolic blessing over you right now:

Father, I ask in the name of Your risen Son, Jesus Christ, that You will richly bless my fellow believer with power and strength in the Holy Spirit! Dear Lord, I pray that You will grant new enlightenment and revelation so that my friend's eyes will be opened even more to the riches of Your glory, power, and unsearchable riches in Christ Jesus. Dear Father in Heaven, will You please liberally pour out the power of Your love and blessing? I pray this with thanksgiving and joy in the name of our Lord and Savior, Jesus Christ. Amen.

Endnotes

1. *Webster's Collegiate Dictionary*, 10th Edition (Springfield, MA: Merriam-Webster, Inc., 1994), p. 122.

2. *Webster's Collegiate Dictionary*, 10th Edition, p. 122.

3. *Strong's*, **blessed** (Hebrew, #835).

4. *Strong's,* **gracious** (drawn from various definitions provided, Hebrew, #2603).

5. R. Laird Harris, Gleason L. Archer, Jr., Bruce K. Waltke, eds., *Theological Wordbook of the Old Testament*, Vol. II (Chicago: Moody Press, 1980) **shem** ("name" #2405), p. 934.

Chapter 7

Discern the Pressures of Progress and Hindrances to Revival

On one fine Sunday morning when I anticipated delivering an important word from the Lord to the church congregation, a church deacon (or steward as we sometimes call them in England) handed me a brown envelope bearing the words "Private and Confidential." If you find yourself chuckling at this point, then undoubtedly you have received similar envelopes before. Sadly, I've learned that they don't usually contain checks (cheques). Now I've learned a few lessons since the morning that first brown envelope arrived, but I was intrigued by this package. *After all*, I thought, *this could be very important! This could be an important prayer request for the Sunday morning meeting.*

Honestly, I had a strong inkling that it was nothing of the sort, but I was *intrigued*. (Stop chuckling if you can.) When I opened this brown envelope, I was impressed by the number of verses that were written on the enclosed letter. However, it only took me a few short moments to realize that my messenger was not necessarily the bearer of good news. I began to read the "prophetic word" enclosed in my surprise package, and it basically said, "You have built on sand, the storms and the winds are going to beat on this house, and great will be the fall of it." This was not what I would term "good news" to receive immediately before a Sunday morning service. (Are you *still* chuckling?)

The problem is that I had fallen victim to a manipulator, and part of the hook on a manipulator's fishing line is the enticing thought, *Well, I don't want to miss the Word of the Lord.* Church and ministry leaders normally want to be open to input from fellow believers, and we want to be vulnerable to the Spirit. That morning I found myself thinking, *Now I've got to lead a meeting in a few moments, but is God really saying, "You've built on sand, and great will be the fall of this house"*?

I found myself being diverted from the one thing that I was meant to deliver to God's family that morning. This thing even followed me home after the service. The whole day was taken up with doubts and questions like, "Is God happy with me?" When I shared it with my wife, Irene, she sort of smiled as though it wasn't very important. I thought, *Typical.* (Why have you started chuckling again?)

Within a few days, I heard a loud knock at the door and when I opened it, I was met by a very austere gentleman. He solemnly announced (without the slightest hint of a smile), "I've got a word from the Lord for you."

I said, "Is it a good one?" (There you go chuckling again.)

Evidently this man wasn't amused, because he said with even less possibility of a smile showing, "That's not for me to say; I'm only the postman."

I paused a moment, and then foolishly said, "Well, okay, give it to me."

Do you know what he said? He said, "You've built on sand, the storms and the winds are going to beat on this house, and this house is going to fall to the ground."

Being a biblical sort of person, my mind immediately jumped to the verse that says, "Every matter must be established by the testimony of two or three witnesses" (2 Cor. 13:1b). The thought flashed through my mind, *I'm on my way down, and so is the church!* Then I went to Irene and said, "What do you make of this?"

Do you know what she said to me? She said, "Well, they're friends, aren't they?" (You're chuckling again.)

I thought, *It can't be that simple.* Now if there is just one thing you remember from this chapter on how to maintain vision in the midst of pressure, remember this: Beware of brown envelopes marked with the words "Private and Confidential."

Seriously, as I look back on my life and ministry, I remember times when I knew that the call of God was on my life, yet it seemed like I lived in a perpetual fog. It seemed nearly impossible to find direction, purpose, or clarity in the midst of turmoil and opposition. Yet each time, Irene and I learned that through every trial and challenge, God was with us.

If you have embraced the renewal and revival of God, then it is almost certain that you will find yourself in the midst of pressure and difficulty. You will need to embrace some of these pressures once you realize they are necessary components of every life dedicated to going on in Christ. They are signs and confirmation that the Holy Spirit is at work in your life and that God's Presence is making its weight and glory felt.

Most of the pressures that come against us, however, have nothing to do with God. The Lord is calling us to walk in divine wisdom and discernment in our generation. We need to clearly discern what God is calling us to do and what He is *not* calling us to do. Who does He want us to get involved with, and who should be left well enough alone?

We rejoice and thank God for all of the good things He has done in the earth in the last few years—the wonderful outpouring of "the Father's blessing" in Toronto, His visitation in power at Holy Trinity Brompton Anglican Church, His sudden descent in glory on the congregation of Brownsville Assembly of God Church in Pensacola, Florida, and countless other ways He has touched His people with the fires of revival.

In May of 1994, I was personally impacted to the core of my being by the new wave of the Presence and power of God. My family was touched, my church was touched, and within a couple of weeks, it seemed like every pressure just seemed to lift off my shoulders and off the church congregation. Our people were beginning to be optimistic again, and their faces were filled with smiles and great joy. I was especially pleased when I noticed that even our counseling rooms seemed to be empty as people were blessed and delivered from chronic problems of various sorts. There was a secret hope in me that instead of going through the endless cycles of counseling many people went through, that God had come to do away with all that. I thought, *We've died and gone to Heaven*, because all the pastoral pressures had been lifted.

Then reality set in, of course. Before long, we began to realize that even though God was continuing to bless us in renewal and revival, we were still going to face times of pressure, persecution, and difficulty. The Lord opened my eyes to a number of things to help prepare me for long-term revival and harvest, and I want to share three areas of pressure that seem to be common to everyone called to serve as leaders in churches, ministries, and body ministry. The Lord showed me some ways to deal with these kinds of pressure, and how to maintain the vision of God while going through difficulty.

Even as an eight-year-old boy, I had a strange fascination for revival. I believe that God spoke to my heart in those early years that I would one day see genuine revival. I didn't know exactly what it was then, but through the years I sensed that God was calling me to revival again and again. I didn't know exactly what that call would involve, and I found myself facing all kinds of difficulties and pressures. Many times I would seek unity in the Body of Christ, only to be misunderstood and sometimes sidelined or disregarded by others in local church settings.

You and I live in a real world. We may have a powerful vision and direction straight from the heart of God, but we will still have to deal with pressures in three vital areas that threaten to either divert us from God's central call or rob us of our time. They will also effectively rob us of our clarity of thought. These are some of the greatest hindrances to revival we will ever face.

Handling the Pressure of People

Since the Church is composed of people, it is natural to expect that church leaders will face "pressure" or demands from people. Many of those demands or needs are right and proper, and God will provide the grace and ability necessary to meet those needs. Shepherds after all must accept the weight of responsibility for the care of the flock. However, there are ungodly pressures that go far beyond the norm, as far as people are concerned. Most of these "people pressures" come from two particular types of people. I'm a little wiser about these two groups today, and I want to be as practical as I possibly can to help equip you beforehand for this kind of pressure.

1. The Underminer

Every one of us who dares to launch out and fulfill God's purposes in our lives will run into someone who will try to undermine our work and service. Some of these underminers are looking for a better position or a place to start up the ladder of success and respect in the church. They might even be looking at *your* position for themselves. Whatever their motive, the fruit of their undermining ways is the same.

I have to say that I'm a particularly gullible person. I love people, and I believe that God has given me a heart for people. That's why I thank God that I married Irene. If it were not for her, I might be taken in by all kinds of things. On occasion, I've looked at her while describing certain situations and noticed her just shaking her head. That is my cue that I had better listen to her warnings. (You're chuckling again.)

King David had to deal with one of the greatest of all underminers in human history. David had been blessed with a large number of very loyal supporters in his life. He knew the joy of the covenant relationship he shared with Jonathan, but also he knew the heartbreak of betrayal by an underminer. The sad thing about David's situation was that the underminer who nearly destroyed him was his own son, Absalom. Ironically, Absalom's name means "son of safety and peace." The story of Absalom's undermining scheme in Second Samuel 15 reveals a number of traits that every leader in the Church should be watching for.

The Five Deadly Traits of an Underminer

A. *The underminer "provides for himself."* The Bible says, "In the course of time, Absalom *provided himself* with a chariot and horses and with fifty men to run ahead of him" (2 Sam. 15:1). The underminer always looks out for "number one" by gaining the trappings or appearance of importance before it is earned through humble service or genuine accomplishment. This person will outfit him or herself with people and things just to fool the foolish. An underminer majors on exterior appearances rather than on internal qualities. From the beginning, the motives of an underminer are questionable.

B. *The underminer is always ready to "hear complaints."* Absalom grew up around the royal court. He knew how things worked. He got up early and took a position right at the door of the main entrance to the king's court because he knew everyone had to pass by there to see the king. Whenever someone came to lodge a complaint with the king, hoping for a favorable decision, Absalom would call out to him. Absalom *positioned himself* between the people and God's chosen leader. His motive was to become the favorable listening ear, an alternative authority that would better identify with the needs and the burdens of the people (whether they were right or wrong). The goal wasn't justice; it was the throne. He would listen to the complaints and groanings of the people and then say, "Well, *if I were king....*"

In my early years of church ministry, I thought there was a breed of people who seemed to operate in "special" gifts of the Spirit not mentioned in the Scriptures. These mysteriously "gifted" people would come to me and say, "Have you heard about the difficulties in the church?" I would say, "What difficulties specifically?" and they would always reply, "Well, we can't go into details because it's the sort of material that has to be kept in confidence."

"If you're talking about difficulties and problems in the church, then I need a little bit of information," I'd tell them. "I need some names and addresses so I can speak with them."

Then would come the exclusive part of their "gift." They would say, "Well, we're really sorry, but these people have come to us to share the things that are on their hearts, and they shared them in confidence. But we just wanted to tell you: You've got to be careful, because there are all kinds of pressures and problems in the church *that you know nothing about.*" I guess I didn't have their particular gift for hearing complaints. The fruit of such "gifts," of course, is that the peace of God is just stripped away and replaced by fear and heavy burdens. If this happens to you, then you've just been victimized by an underminer.

C. *The underminer "steals the hearts of the people."* The Bible says, "Absalom behaved in this way toward all the Israelites who came to the king asking for justice, and so he stole the hearts of the men of Israel" (2 Sam. 15:6). David won the affections of Israel by risking his life against Goliath, the Philistines, and in countless other battles for the sake of Israel. He had earned their respect with a lifetime of sacrifice, godly leadership, and diligence in his duties as king. Absalom stole their hearts by whispering pleasing lies and compliments into their ears, mixed with sly accusations against his own father—something Israelites are taught to abhor from birth. Yet the people yielded their allegiance to Absalom for the cheap price of four years' worth of a turncoat's sweet lies. The worst betrayals and most effective thefts always come from those you love and trust. We can't stop loving and trusting, but we can exercise godly discernment.

D. *The underminer will begin to "act politically."* God's Word says of Absalom: "Also, whenever anyone approached him to bow down before him, Absalom would reach out his hand, take hold of him and kiss him" (2 Sam. 15:5).

Absalom worked hard to convince people that he would make a better king than his father. Yet when the people would try to bow down to him to express their awe and respect, then he would pull the supreme political maneuver. He wouldn't let them bow down to him. Instead he would quickly grab their hand and give them an affectionate kiss—as if they were beloved insiders. He made the people he'd duped think they were regarded as "trusted equals" and confidantes to "the man who would be king." Flattery by any other name is still flattery.

Absalom's persistent deception at the king's gate finally paid dividends. The Bible says, "And so the conspiracy gained strength, and Absalom's following kept on increasing" (2 Sam. 15:12b).

We need to recognize the traits of underminers early, before damage is done in Christ's Body. No, we don't need to launch some kind of witch hunt or stop trusting people. We simply need clarity and discernment. We need to look more for the *right person* rather than for the *wrong person*. I call it looking for the *underliners* instead of the *underminers*. David had Jonathan in his life for a time. This man was always submitting to and underlining the ministry of David.

2. The Manipulator

I call the second group "the manipulators." Manipulators are people who want to take our time for themselves, and time is very precious. I hope to bring peace to everyone involved in pastoral ministry and counseling. All too often, pastors and counselors find themselves locked into endless hours of seemingly useless and unproductive "listening" ministry. When they emerge, they feel like *they* are the ones who need counseling and prayer! I've often spent too much time with people who perhaps I shouldn't have. As a result, I wasn't always able to allocate quality time to those who have consistently supported and blessed the work of God.

Signs and Symptoms of Manipulation

Before we look at some of the types of manipulators we are likely to encounter in the Church, I want to provide some common signs or symptoms of manipulation. How do you know when manipulation is taking place? What kind of things should you look for? It is difficult to know whether a person is being genuine or not, but the following signs and symptoms will help us discern if there are elements of manipulation present.

If you sense that your time is being wasted, you are probably being manipulated. Trust your inner witness. Sometimes I'll begin to talk with someone who had made an appointment, and while I'm sitting there listening to the conversation, I'll begin to have an inward sense that time is being wasted—*my time.* Very often this sense comes when the counselee gets lost in a circular argument or unending narrative of woe, bitterness, or confusion. If you can't even begin to grasp what the actual issue is behind the person's endless dialogue, then someone's time is being wasted—yours.

If you suddenly feel tired for no logical reason, then your time is being wasted. Have you ever been in a counseling situation in which someone is unloading his or her heart on you, when all of a sudden you realize you're not really in the room. Naturally, you will probably begin to feel guilty about not giving quality time, but suddenly you may begin to feel very tired for no known reason. This doesn't apply if you failed to go to sleep at a decent hour the night before, but if sleep isn't your problem and you're unnaturally tired in the midst of a ministry situation, look for signs of manipulation. Whenever I run into counselees who are in a manipulative mode, I'll feel a sudden tiredness come over me as they speak. They make me feel as though the weight of the world has suddenly begun to press down on my head. Take action, my friend. You are under the influence of a manipulator.

Anytime someone says, *"You are my last resort,"* you are being manipulated. Beware of any person who tells you, "I've been everywhere else. I've been through counseling, but no one can help. I've been to this person, but he couldn't help me either. You are my last hope."

Most pastors will readily identify with these signs and symptoms of manipulation. They deal with them on a week-to-week or even a day-to-day basis at times. It can put you into an early grave if you let it. Now it is important for us to understand that *manipulation is not always intentional.* As leaders, we need to be able to discern what's going on. The problem is that once God calls us to a particular task, we often get so distracted and entangled with other issues, situations, burdens, and pressures, that we get diverted from the path God called us to take.

Everyone in the Body of Christ needs to talk to someone about difficult issues at times. Obviously a pastor is supposed to care for and love each member of the local flock, but it is not always appropriate for the clock to tick by while the overall ministry is side-lined and idled for hours on end, day after day, over the chronic needs of one person. With the great harvest so near at hand, every minister and church worker must learn how to discern signs of manipulation.

I don't want to depress you further, but let me outline a number of manipulators whom I have come across. At times, I have found elements of manipulation in my own behavior, and it is probably safe to say the same of everyone. However, when these things become so extreme that they dominate a person's behavior, there is danger ahead for the victim and for everyone who deals with him or her. It is vitally important for God's leaders to give themselves solely to what God has called them!

The Five Faces Of the Manipulator

A. *The emotional manipulator* normally comes to you with a comment like this: "Nobody cares. Nobody loves me." These manipulators will often support their claim with unfounded comments like, "The problem with this church is that there's no love here! No one will give me any space. They won't even give me the time of day." This immediately begins to pull on *your* life. Why? If you fail to give them space, then you feel that you are proving their point. If you fail to care at the level they expect you to care, then you are underlining just how "uncaring" the church really is.

B. *The super-spiritual manipulator* will probably come to you with the stock comment, "God told me…" This manipulator loves brown envelopes bearing the words "Private and Confidential." The difficulty with these situations is summed up in the question, "What if God *really did* tell this person something of importance?"

One time someone phoned me from another country and said, "God told me that I'm to be on your team." I said, "That's really nice—*who are you?*" (You're chuckling again.) I was baffled. I couldn't understand why someone would pull a stunt like that. The answer is always very simple to the manipulator: "Well, God told me." My answer has become just as simple: "Perhaps God may have told you, but He didn't tell me."

I've learned that super-spiritual manipulators like to wrap their divine conclusions in endless layers of Scripture verses, as if this makes their case even stronger. Now as leaders in the community of Christ, we want to be open to the Spirit. We want to be able to hear His voice—even if hard or difficult words are brought to us. The most important key to discerning the validity of such "prophetic words" is summed up in one question you should always ask yourself: "Is it true?" Once you press through and discern by the Spirit whether a thing is true or not, you will be lifted away from the influence of manipulative behavior.

C. You may encounter *the demonized manipulator* once in a lifetime, but at least you will be prepared and forewarned. Paul had to deal with a demonized manipulator who followed him all over Philippi in Acts 16:16-18. Her constant harassment and jabbering irritated Paul so much that he finally turned around and cast the demon of divination out of her. Most ministers aren't as discerning today. Sadly, I've been to a number of churches who allowed their God-given vision to be halted because of demonic manipulation.

This reminds me of the day my family was held at bay by an elderly demonized manipulator. This was the only time I've run into this kind of situation, and it was scary business until my eyes were opened to the root of the problem. A lady in her 60's came to me and said, "Unless you help me, I'm lost." (That should have been my cue right there, but I didn't know then what I know now.) I did think, *That's a bit of a strong statement to begin with,* however.

I was intrigued by the urgency expressed by this elderly lady and I wanted to help her. She proceeded to unload an entire lifestyle and life history of problems onto my aching shoulders. These weren't minor difficulties; they were satanic things. I made matters worse by making some major mistakes. I devoted too much time to this woman. Her needs appeared so desperate that my concern became almost compulsive. I felt that I had to see her free. It was as though the pressure of this lady's problems became stronger and more pressing than all the pressures in the church combined! I began to hear this lady's voice running in my mind constantly. She would phone in the middle of the night and say, "You've got to help me. If you don't help me, I'll die!"

Finally the day came when I found this woman standing outside our family home. She said, *"I'm not leaving here until you help me!"* I'm not proud of this, but I have to admit that for two weeks, we found ourselves—as a family—afraid and fearful of an elderly lady who was pressuring us on every occasion with her constant demands and comments. This woman had a little yellow "mini," a tiny English car, and *even her registration plate read "B-A-D."* Okay, you can laugh about that, but my point is this: We were getting robbed of our time, our sanity, and our priorities. For a time, even my family was held hostage by that woman's demonic manipulation. I allowed myself to be robbed without knowing it and diverted from what God had called me to do. Finally I understood the demonic root of the problem and broke her manipulative and demonic grip on my family and ministry—a much wiser and more cautious man.

D. *The inadequate manipulator* is driven by the pain of rejection to constantly seek attention and approval from leadership figures. Of course these people really do need attention and loving care, but it is important to recognize and deal with any manipulative behavior early in the ministry process. Only then can true deliverance and healing begin.

E. *The unintentional manipulator* is overeager to "launch his or her ministry." These individuals desperately want to serve the Lord—preferably from a very visible position. They may tell you, "I'm looking for full-time ministry, and you're the way it's going to come." Their manipulation is genuinely unintentional, and there is no doubt that they are zealous of heart. Yet the manipulation is real, and it is out of order. It can exert very real pressure on your personal ministry and life. If you are not careful, even an unintentional manipulator can hold you back from the things God called you to do.

Big-hearted pastoral-type people in particular need discernment in the way they handle people. We all need to learn how to recognize the telltale traits of the "underminers" who so often sink deadly roots in local church bodies. We also need to watch out for signs of manipulation and at least ask some questions to make sure we're not just sucked in to endless hours of listening and talking that lead nowhere. Only those who seriously want to be free are worthy of our time— even Jesus can't (and won't) help those who don't want freedom. We need to learn how to *handle the pressure of people*.

Be Aware of the Pressure of Programs

It is important for every church leader to "get space." I am referring to our need for physical, mental, and spiritual separation from the day-to-day grind of ministry from time to time. Jesus thought this was so important that He often left His disciples to spend entire nights alone on a mountain in prayer, solitude, reflection, and peaceful communion with His Father. The results are astounding.

Church life sometimes seems to go in cycles. Not too long ago before the fires of renewal and revival ignited in our church, we were saying, "We need to cut back our meetings. We have entirely too many meetings! We need to spend time with our families, our friends, and our relatives." Then God's Presence overwhelmed our meetings, and suddenly we had even *more* meetings, hours and hours of thoroughly fantastic meetings that lasted into the early morning. Then we said, "We thought we were going to cut back, and now it seems God is pressing us forward. We're spending even more hours in ministry!"

It is important to recognize the pressure that programs can produce. Every leader has to deal with pressure to keep up with the status quo, which is usually in conflict with the constant pressure from the Holy Spirit to remain flexible and open to change. There is a wind of change in our generation, isn't there? At times, I've felt a little bit like Isaac who would dig precious wells in dry country, only to discover that his handiwork had become a point of envy, jealousy, dispute, and disharmony as his enemies would come and fill in his wells (see Gen. 26:20). Much of my life I've been digging wells and finding they're being filled in. Sometimes you dig a well and find opposition. Other times you dig a well and find yourself in a dispute.

Today, I'm thrilled to tell you that, like Isaac, I've dug a well called Rehoboth (meaning "a broad place"[1]) and I'm finding some *space*. God is also giving "space" to the local church. What do I mean by "space"? I have space when "the filling of my time is not dictated by outward pressures or circumstances." I have space when my time isn't taken up by issues that come from outside and dictate the way that I do things.

When church programs suddenly seem to expand, we need to find space and room. Every leader has to learn how to push things to the periphery at times just to get hold of what God is calling him to.

The apostles faced this problem in Acts 6, when the Church suddenly exploded with thousands of new converts, and the needs of the people weren't always being met. The apostles knew they were called to give themselves to prayer and the Word, but were being inundated with the practical details of caring for the needy. Something had to give—they needed space. So they appointed godly people to take care of the needs of the people and the early Church continued its progress.

How Do We Get Room?

Church leaders must find space or room to pursue their central calling from God. I want to be free to move in the sphere and the gifts that God has called me to. We must reserve time exclusively for seeking the face of God and for studying His Word. We need to find space in the midst of pressure, and that isn't always easy. Here are six ways I've discovered to help me make room in the midst of pressure:

1. *Learn how to manage your time* (instead of allowing other people, circumstances, and outside pressures to do it for you). Don't let your appointment of calendar or diary dictate the things you do and when you do them. Maintain control over the allocation of your time and energy and learn how to manage yourself! This is one of the most important keys to leadership in the midst of pressure.

2. *Create support structures.* I have been blessed with some wonderful people who are willing to take the strain of leadership from my shoulders through delegation. Moses did it. Jesus did it. The 11 apostles did it in the

Book of Acts. Paul did it in the churches he planted. Find trustworthy people and duplicate yourself in them. The only way to pursue the mission of the Church and achieve breakthrough toward your vision is to create biblical support structures.

3. *Throw off entanglements.* For a time, I began to think that Christian ministry was like "knitting with fog." I knew that God had called me, but I felt like I was waving my arms uselessly trying to break through the fog. It took me almost a year, but by God's grace I was finally able to recognize and throw off entanglements. Frankly, this anointing move of the Spirit over the Church has brought miraculous answers to some of that fog-clearing business. One of the most notable examples is Muriel's experience in the Lord, and the way it united our congregation after years of difficulties stemming from our first decision to merge two distinct churches and leadership teams together. If you seek Him, then God, by His Holy Spirit, will help you throw off the entanglements, the things that grip you, so you can break through.

4. *Assess the unimportant.* Are you doing things that God never told you to do? Stop, look, listen, and then say, "This is what I need to be doing, not these things. This is what I'm called to." Don't waste your days grappling with the unimportant.

5. *Stop ineffective meetings.* Don't be surprised if you discover a small contingent that feels God doesn't want you to stop certain meetings (ministry and administrative meetings). One thing is certain for human beings—change is difficult. Nevertheless, we have to

allow the wind of the Spirit to blow through our structures and programs.

6. *Learn how to say no.* If you are motivated by needs, then you will be running here and there and everywhere until you drop dead before your time. Learn how to say "no" to *everything* God hasn't called you to do. Jesus didn't heal everyone every time—He only ministered as His Father directed. Nothing more, nothing less.

Recognize the Pressure of Progress

Whenever you move forward and serious growth comes, don't expect the pressures you face to decrease—expect them to increase. Progress produces pressure. There's no way around it. That doesn't mean you should avoid progress; it means you need to *share your burdens.*

It doesn't take a genius to realize that we need to think very seriously about growth in the light of God's unprecedented move across the earth today. I was brought up in the Methodist church, and I have to admit that in my situation, we never expected too much—and we weren't disappointed. We're living in different times. God is moving and people are being set free. I believe God is invading entire nations with the power of His Spirit, and He is blowing fiercely on all our church structures. Those that are built on the sand of man, or the old "one man, one general, one star" model, will quickly collapse under the pressures of genuine revival. If Jesus rejected this model, then we should too. (Frankly, if you want an easy life, then stop praying for revival.)

If you want revival, then you need to learn how to delegate and share your leadership burdens. Share your vision and direction, and devote yourself to training and equipping new leaders. I don't personally feel that God expects existing leaders to step aside for new ones to come. No, I believe He's saying, "Move onward and upward so others can come in." The role of existing leaders is to train and equip new leaders to accommodate progress.

Endnotes

1. *Strong's,* **Rehoboth** (Hebrews, #7344).

Chapter 8

Building a Team

From Genesis to Revelation, God's Word portrays ministry and leadership as a team activity. Yes, one person always takes the lead in things, but that person never seems to act alone. Adam and Eve were the first team. Now Adam did go it alone for a time, but after God watched him mope around for awhile, He finally decreed, "It is not good for the man to be alone. I will make a helper suitable for him" (Gen. 2:18). Adam had no trouble staying busy after that.

Noah had a family team, and so did Abraham. Most of the judges of Israel had teams of sorts, but some, like Samson, took a hard fall because they associated with and depended on undependable people as confidantes and partners.

Moses has often been celebrated as the ultimate model of "one-man leadership" in certain church circles. The fact is that he started out as a team leader and was later openly rebuked for gravitating to the one-man mode of leadership and nearly burning out. He immediately began to delegate his responsibilities and authority, and God blessed him in the work. The prophets interacted with one another, with assistants and students, and with family members.

David was forced to start his leadership career alone when he was abandoned in the sheep fields by family, and when he was forced to stand for God alone in the battlefield while his nation's king and assembled soldiers watched. He overcame lions, bears, and giants by pressing through in partnership with God to became perhaps the greatest team leader in the Bible. David went into the cave Adullam a loser, where he was joined by more "losers." He emerged from the cave and exile years later with perhaps the best trained, unified, and effective fighting force in the Near East. It was from this "team" that David drew his "mighty men of renown," men who exercised delegated authority at his side for the rest of his life. Solomon, despite his wisdom, defied God's Word and his father's advice and created a team of thousands of godless wives and concubines that ultimately brought his kingdom down in the ruin and shame born of idolatry.

In the New Testament, Jesus Christ Himself chose to operate with a team provided by His Father, and His disciples after Him continued that pattern through the first century. The apostle Paul developed this apostolic team concept to a refined degree in his church-planting ministry. And though the "one-man rule" became popular in the Church after the death of the apostles, it seems unlikely that God would so abruptly change the pattern He established so carefully in both the Old and New Testaments. The unsavory fruit of many of these "one-man" models of church leadership in ancient times and today seems to further support the validity of God's original plan for *team leadership* in the Church.

My earliest team ministry experiences began when I spent several years traveling with a four-man music ministry team from the British Youth for Christ. Later on, I ended up in a church-planting situation where, for a period of time, I found that I had to personally handle most of the details, labor, and administration of the thing. Since we had just a small nucleus of people, I often found myself playing taxi driver, putting on the heating system before the meetings, setting out chairs, and doing many other things on my own. At that point, I felt it very important that we start to build teams.

As the church began to grow, we found ourselves in a larger church situation with numerous departments and nearly 600 people. That is when we started to develop team dynamics (teams within teams) in every area of church life and ministry. A little later in my experience, we started to develop apostolic team ministry, where people with extra-local ministry committed themselves to serve a group of churches within a larger network of churches.

I have found that the same principles of team ministry apply with a group of four people as with a congregation of hundreds or thousands. What is a *team*? The term became a Church "buzz word" for a time, and people thought, *Well, if you didn't have a team, then you've got to find one—or pretend.* Unfortunately a lot of people pretended, because they weren't really in a team. They were simply doing their own thing while talking team language.

The first dictionary definition of *team* I found is this: "A set of workers or players."[1] Straight away we are thrust into the concept of plurality. You can't have a team of one. The second definition of *team* is "two or more beasts of burden harnessed together."[2] The concept easily applies to people, local church bodies, and the Church worldwide joined together *for a purpose.* They move something by pulling in the same direction and by working together. Now if team dynamics fail along the way, if we try to shift the burden from one man to many people too quickly and find ourselves going in different directions, then the one-man ministry model may seem to be more of a blessing than the biblical team concept!

Thirdly, the dictionary said that a *team* is "a united or concerted effort as distinguished from individual work."[3] This gets us into the whole area of motives in ministry, where we understand, "It's not just my agenda that matters; we own this thing together as a corporate body." Obviously we can contribute to the mix, but team ministry in the local church or evangelistic outreach is a *joint effort* in which other people's viewpoints are heard. Yes, there must and should be a central leader, but a true team is marked by united or concerted effort as distinguished from individual work.

A *team* is also "a group of people organized to work together."[4] Here we throw in that little word, *organized*, because for teams to really function, there has to be an element of organization.

A team is composed of a set or group of people who are in some way harnessed together, who are going in the same direction, and who very often have a weight to pull as they go in that direction. There is an element of organization that joins them together so that they know who they are, where they're going, and why. They recognize that it's not their own personal agenda that matters, or else they would be off seeing to their own affairs.

The Benefits of Working in a Team

Why should we operate in a team? Is it just the latest thing to do? Is it the newest church picture or the latest craze in trendy church government? I have found eight proven reasons for working as a team in God's Kingdom.

1. *It is clearly seen in Scripture.* The Godhead itself is our supreme source of community. Is it accidental or coincidental that God chooses to operate as a team in the persons of God the Father, God the Son, and God the Holy Spirit? These three work as one in total

cooperation, love, appreciation, and submission. I realize that we are thinking rather humanly here about One who is sublime, but all the dynamics of team relationships are found in the eternal Godhead.

The New Testament is filled with teams of people in ministry and service. Jesus ministered with His disciples and was with them virtually around the clock for three years. Paul the apostle formed apostolic teams, and operated in great flexibility. He didn't go into places on his own, but tended to work with a constantly changing mixture of people to raise up ministers for local church bodies. The New Testament paints broad pictures of highly flexible and adaptable apostolic bands, teams, and pluralities of elders specifically described in Jerusalem and in many or most of the churches Paul planted.

You will always find that elders oversaw local fellowships in New Testament Church structures. The whole concept of a pastor leading a flock is quite foreign to the picture of the New Testament Church. Instead, you very often see elders overseeing and ruling the Church. So the whole concept, I believe, of *team*, is very clearly a scriptural concept. It's clearly seen in Scripture.

2. *It makes room for a variety of gifts and abilities to develop.* However good, clever, or blessed a person may be, he or she will never be able to carry all the gifts that are necessary in church life or for the task he or she is called to do. It's not because of man; it's because of God's plan. Man's churches seem to be built around personalities. Perhaps their founding pastor is a great Bible teacher, an expositor, a speaker, or a charismatic leader. The fact is that God planned to distribute His gifts "severally as He wills" to whomever He

wants, without input or approval from us. Jesus alone possessed all the gifts and fruits of the Spirit. In our day, we have to be content with possessing all these gifts through our unity and interdependence on one another.

3. *It allows the weakness of one to be covered by the strengths of another.* I think that it is vitally important for me to have people alongside me who are actually stronger or more effective in some areas than I am! On our local pastoral team, we have a brilliant man who was a lecturer with the Assemblies of God Bible College. He is far better than the rest of us with regard to theological issues, and I can tell you that he is a great blessing. When people ask for in-depth answers for questions like, "What does the Bible teach on divorce?" I just say, "Well, ask John Phillips." I know he has a gift and the resources to effectively (and quickly) answer a question that could pull me away from my central calling. Also, Chris Bowater oversees our worship department, which means I now don't have to lead the worship. They are able to cover my weaknesses.

Of course, this is where we get to the nitty-gritty. If I'm honest, I have to say there have been times in my life when I've thought, *Well, of course, I want to be part of a team where everybody does well. But I'd rather that they didn't do **too well**, you know, because if they do extra especially well, then that leaves me rather vulnerable.*

Sadly, some people try to build a team by carefully choosing people who are actually not as good as they are in particular areas. That way these "team members" won't shine too brightly, and they will simply make the leader look good (as all good "yes people" must do). That is not a team at all. In a strong team, my weaknesses will be covered by the strengths of someone else on the team, and vice versa.

4. *It is important for us to be accountable.* I am even more grateful for our leadership team as our local church life proceeds deeper into revival and the Spirit of God. I am living so close to people in covenant relationship that none of us can "get away with stuff" for very long before we are called into account by loving friends and team members. The closer you get in terms of relationship, the more genuine accountability becomes a practical reality in your life.

A major problem contributing directly to nearly every "fall" of prominent Christian leaders in the last decade is that leaders often feel that they are exempt from accountability. Leaders, more than anyone else, need someone to speak into their lives and hold them personally accountable for their motives, actions, and decisions. I believe the team concept from God's Word is the ideal model for accountability rooted in open and vulnerable relationships in Christ.

5. *It provides an ideal environment for learning.* Participation and commitment to a team provides the finest and most effective vehicle on the face of the earth for the formation of Christlike character.

My first exposure to team ministry occurred during my early 20's when I traveled with a team of musicians called "The Advocates" for British Youth for Christ during an era I try to forget about. We were together through thick and thin for three years as we ministered all over Europe. I found that that period in my life was very "character-forming."

The team of four was led by my cousin, Dave Kitchen, who was older than me. I began to think that Dave always seemed to land in the nicest house at the end of a ministry trip or travel day. If there was a bad place, I got it. One time I was stuck in a room filled with shelves of weird New Age books, and over my head was mounted a big ram's head with a snake around it. Across from me there was a big curved sword, and there were occult symbols all over the room! I went into this room and thought, *These are not Christians!* I had a wonderful night, as you can imagine. Things got worse the following morning when Cousin Dave told me about the wonderful place he landed in.

Another time my host said, "We are redecorating the place." I could tell. There was no carpet on the floor, and there were no curtains. Then she said, "You know, you'll have to get undressed in the dark." I thought, *Well, I suppose worse things can happen than this.* My "bed" was an inflatable air mattress. I thought, *Well, praise God for air matresses*, but just as I was about to go to sleep, I heard a knock on the door. My host stuck her arm inside the door to drop an air pump on the floor. "By the way, you'll need this in the night." Something worse *had* come along. All through the night, I had to get up and pump up my leaking air bed. I was especially happy to see Cousin Dave the next morning.

Finally I demanded that *I choose* accommodations the next go round, and David agreed (even the best teams will have confrontation occasionally). We were in Holland at the time, and of the four choices available, I took choice number three. As I'm getting out of the van, I saw Cousin Dave's smiling face in the wing mirror—it was a kind of sickly Charismatic grin. Immediately I thought, *He's seen something that I haven't.* Hindsight is 20/20. Although it was a very hot summer's day by European standards, I saw a blazing fire in the fireplace as

I walked closer to the house. Hunched in front of the fire was a man bundled up in a hat, scarf, and coat. I thought, *This is typical. I've done it again.*

I was met by two elderly hosts who could not speak a word of English. We managed to while away the rest of the very warm afternoon with various signs and sounds. Evening came around and we were still trying to make conversation the best we could. When bedtime arrived, I was thinking, *Well, praise the Lord!*

I climbed up a flight of stairs with this little elderly couple, wondering why they were giggling and pointing. Then I realized they were pointing to a step ladder leading through a small opening in the ceiling. When I started to climb this step ladder with my suitcase in my hand, my humorous hosts suddenly shook their heads and I gathered it wasn't possible to get my suitcase through the opening. I thought, *What would they like me to do?* I understood through their sign language that I was to go into a nearby room to put on my pajamas before climbing the ladder.

There are worse things in life than putting on your pajamas and climbing step ladders, I thought. I was getting a bit philosophical by that point. Once I'd put on my pajamas, I began climbing up the step ladder toward a trap door. When I opened the door, I found to my amazement that this so-called room was about the size of a coffin! (I'm serious.) After some serious body contortions, I finally settled into bed with the ceiling about six inches away from my nose. Honestly, when I shut the trap door, I thought, *This could be the last anybody ever sees of me. I don't even know the Dutch word for help!* As I lay there in my coffin bed in the stifling attic of that quaint house in Holland, I was thinking, *Well, at least I can thank the Lord I'm not claustrophobic.*

I tell can you that in that moment of time, God spoke to me. I really feel God had placed me in a position where I actually said to Him, "Lord, I've come to the point where there are certain things You're wanting to deal with in my character. I want to repent of my wrong attitudes, and I am thankful, Lord, that it's only one night. Would You please forgive me for my attitude toward my dear cousin Dave? Lord, the best I know how, I want to be grateful wherever You put me in the future."

6. *It combats individualism and pride.* When you're walking together with people, you learn to trust one another and look beyond the end of your strengths and recognize one another's weaknesses. It deals a blow to issues of pride and individualism. You begin to say, "We're walking and working together. We're pulling this load together." I think there's nothing better than team life.

7. *It diminishes the possibility of burnout or disillusionment.* Just in the small city of Lincoln, I have seen three minister friends (and good people) in denominational structures who literally burned out. They are no longer in the ministry. I believe that participation in a true team diminishes the possibility of burnout and disillusionment.

8. *It allows for flexibility and development.* The Church is dynamic and constantly growing and changing. We face a real danger in seeing our teams becoming fixed in "concrete" in terms of structure. Every team must remain open to change, and be adaptable and flexible. Our relationships should never become possessive.

Choosing a Team

Following are some some very practical points I've gleaned the hard way about choosing members of a team.

1. *Ask yourself, "What is the reason for us being together?"* No team should be formed just to form a team. Every true team has a vital reason for being. What is the team trying to do? Where is it heading? Is it to oversee the church? Is it to provide pastoral care? What is its purpose?

2. *There must be a recognized leader.* Some churches prefer a "collegium of elders" approach in which no one person is in leadership. Some churches run effectively like that. Personally, I have found that teams work best when there is a recognized leader. I am not talking about a dictator; I am talking about a "chief among equals" on a team composed entirely of *servant leaders*. A true ministry team of servant leaders isn't composed of "leaders who serve," but of "servants who lead." It is easy to work as a team under this kind of recognized leader.

Without a recognized leader to move things along, you'll often end up in deadlocks because no one will take the initiative despite an entire day devoted to endless discussion. To avoid conflict, you will find yourselves being so nice to one another that no decisions will be made. The team dynamic needs leadership to function properly. The team leader should be someone who is unafraid to make choices after carefully considering all the opinions and data whenever the team is unable to decide effectively.

3. *There must be much prayer.* Jesus only chose His disciples after spending a whole night in prayer. There was a sense of waiting on the Father to rightly discern God's choice for the people assigned His Son's "team." I wonder how much prayer and waiting on God goes into some of the structures that we put together? We often choose the easiest way or the "politically correct" path for choosing team members, but we can avoid a lot of problems and pain if we will pray and hear God before we choose team members.

4. *The assembling of a team must be the joining of friends— not just gifted people.* Team members should be a group of friends who are *joined together by the Lord.* Don't go for just gifted people; look for loyal people who are committed to one another.

5. *There must be a time of proving.* More and more, we are not just saying, "Would you do this task?" We are putting a time frame on leadership tasks, especially early in the formation process. We may ask someone to help in a situation and assess how he or she approaches the task in a time of proving before the person's selection to a more permanent leadership role on a team.

6. *Recognize the gifts in people and release them to minister and serve in their areas of strength.* Allow people to find their places, and once the qualifications for relationship and covenant commitment are met, try to bring them onto a team for specific purposes based on their gifting and ability.

7. *Honor one another.* I'm not talking about just being buddies together; I'm talking about honoring one another. Too often we hear little snipes or side comments

made about brothers and sisters, and it grieves God. We need to speak well of and honor one another. We need to build one another up with encouragement and honor, because leadership responsibility automatically means that we will take some hard hits from time to time.

The Four Dynamics of Team Ministry

Now we need to look at the even more practical issue of team dynamics. What I am going to say may be relatively provocative, because I've found that the issues that divide us are *not* usually theological. Nowhere is this more graphically displayed than in one of the most prominent ministry teams in the Old Testament. You may be thinking, *What Old Testament ministry team could he possibly have found?* Team ministry is not a new concept at all. First I want to take you to an obscure verse in the Book of Micah that says, "I brought you up out of Egypt and redeemed you from the land of slavery. I sent Moses to lead you, also Aaron and Miriam" (Mic. 6:4).

If we were asked, "Who brought the children of Israel out of Egypt?" most of us would say, "Moses." Micah the prophet sets us straight and says that God sent a *team* composed of Moses, *as well as Aaron and Miriam.* Due to the unbelief of the Israelites, God also added a second generation leader named Joshua into the leadership mix. Let's look briefly at the team dynamics between Moses, Aaron, Miriam, and Joshua, to see the interplay that takes place in their respective ministry roles to fulfill God's purposes. Exodus chapters 4 through 6 describe four key dynamics in the team leadership process.

1. *The problem of working alone.* As early as Genesis 2:18, God said, "It is not good for the man to be alone." Obviously God's Word is still true. There are still some horror stories of men in their 70's who never

ever had a "real friend" in terms of ministry. They often felt that they couldn't even share with their wives the things that were going on in their ministerial lives. Bible colleges used to teach young would-be ministers, "If you are a man of God, then you just trust the Lord. You have to go it alone. Trust no one." God is correcting that grave error.

Moses must have felt alone much of his life. He was born in a foreign land, separated from family, and raised in a royal household by a stranger, totally aloof from common men. He named his first son Girshom, which means, "I've become an alien in a foreign land." God changed all that when He met Moses in the "backside of the desert." God often allows people to go through circumstances to work vital principles into their lives. Moses was learning that it is not good for man to be alone.

God met Moses, spoke to him about his assignment, and promptly brought someone into his life as a team member—his own brother, Aaron. When God sent Moses a friend and a brother in the desert, He used a very strong word to describe their meeting: "The Lord said to Aaron, 'Go into the desert to meet Moses.' So he met Moses at the mountain of God and kissed him" (Ex. 4:27). This is what I call the kissing of God, the joining of hearts. No matter how good you may be as an evangelist or pastor, it's not good for you to be on your own.

2. *The complimenting of strengths and weaknesses.* When God told Moses that he was to deliver Israel from Pharaoh, the Bible says, "Moses said to the Lord, 'O Lord, I have never been eloquent, neither in the past

nor since You have spoken to Your servant. I am slow of speech and tongue' " (Ex. 4:10). Moses claimed that he wasn't a good communicator—and God wasn't happy about it. He knew that Moses *would be* a good speaker if he would trust God, but He added someone to Moses' team who was a communicator—Aaron the mouthpiece.

Why didn't God just choose Aaron for the job in the first place? Because the job called for more than honed communication skills—it called for spiritual discernment, strength of character, and conviction. Aaron's weakness showed up when he let the Israelites pressure him into making a golden idol for them to worship while Moses was on a mountain with God! Aaron was weak where Moses was strong.

What about the other two members? The Bible says, "Then Miriam *the prophetess*, Aaron's sister, took a tambourine in her hand, and all the women *followed* her, with tambourines and dancing" (Ex. 15:20). Miriam possessed specific prophetic gifts that were released into the life of the ministry team. She spontaneously led all of Israel in prophetic praise in what is called "The Song of Moses," a prophetic lyric that is still sung by fervent Jews around the world!

Miriam was a prophetic team member who inspired people to follow her right into high worship and praise. Many people today would call her a "psalmist" because her prophetic office or calling expressed itself through music and the arts. God specifically included Miriam in His leadership team because her gifts were important compliments to the mix of strengths and weaknesses in leadership.

This picture of balance and harmony would seem to be the ideal ministry—if all things were to remain the same. The problem is that people often aren't content to do the same things all their lives (and God doesn't always ask us to either—He just wants us to get our direction from Him, not our personal agendas).

3. *The pressures of shared ministry.* The Scriptures are very honest, and they talk bluntly about the difference between theory and practical application. Sometimes things go wrong. Shared ministry has its own set of pressures.

   a. The first pressure was the *authority* of Moses. "Then the Lord said to Moses, 'See, I have made you like God to Pharaoh, and your brother Aaron will be your prophet' " (Ex. 7:1). Whether we like it or not, *God delegates authority as He chooses, with or without our consent.* What do you think Aaron thought when God said his younger brother would be viewed as a god to Pharaoh and that Aaron would be his prophet? That's pretty strong language. Everything will go well as long as Aaron wants to be his elevated brother's prophet. The reality is that Aaron was on a collision course with the pressure of the authority of Moses. In Exodus chapters 7 and 8, Moses would receive direction from God, who would tell Moses, "Tell Aaron..." to do such and such. That was pretty exciting stuff up to a point. At what point do you think Aaron began to think, *Hey, wait a minute. I'm the one holding the staff, arguing with these wizard people, and telling off Pharaoh. When will I get the credit?*

The beauty of this kind of dynamic is that the glory was never meant to go to Moses or to Aaron. The glory is meant to go to God alone. In Church dynamic, it's not *who* is leading or doing this and that—it is God who is working extraordinary things through very ordinary people! He gives authority as He chooses, but you can only have authority if you've submitted to authority.

b. The second kind of pressure from shared ministry is *the pressure of delegation and responsibility* (sometimes called "the Jethro principle"). In Exodus 18:17, Moses' father-in-law, Jethro, visited him and said, "What you are doing is not good." Moses had allowed the weight of leading more than a million people to weigh him down with pressure and too many responsibilities. Jethro told Moses to delegate that responsibility to proven leaders among the Israelites. It is vitally important in the team dynamic that we develop the ability to delegate responsibility and authority to others to relieve the pressures of shared ministry. The apostles in the early Church recognized this need and acted decisively *after much prayer* by appointing spiritual men to serve the people as deacons.

c. *The changing face of shared ministry.* Most of us don't like change, but God is always moving forward, so we have to move with Him. That guarantees that we must *change*.

As the days turned into weeks in the desert, pressures began to mount. Perhaps the leadership team suddenly realized that they were no longer spring chickens. They were all eligible for senior citizen discounts, and they still hadn't managed to reach the Promised Land, thanks to numerous rebellions and delays due to unbelief. That would bring pressure, wouldn't it?

These pressures came to a very dramatic head when Miriam, the elder sister of this family team, decided to step outside her God-given boundary of authority to challenge Moses for the chief position in Numbers 12. Miriam used her brother's interracial marriage as a pretext for the challenge, and she drew Aaron into the gripe session. There were no theological concerns here, just old-fashioned jealousy.

Miriam and Aaron began to talk against Moses because of his Cushite wife, for he had married a Cushite. "Has the Lord spoken only through Moses?" they asked. "Hasn't He also spoken through us?" And the Lord heard this (Numbers 12:1-2).

Perhaps Miriam was upset over the presence of "another woman" coming into the picture as an influence in Moses' life. Maybe she feared Zipporah would mess up the dynamics of the team. Whatever she thought, when she decided to gossip and slander Moses, *she forgot that God was listening.* She compared herself to Moses (it is *always* a mistake to compare yourself to others), and she was saying, in effect, "What's he got that I don't have?" Meanwhile, Aaron, the talkative follower, followed along.

The problem was that Moses wasn't leading because he decided he'd make the best leader. He was leading because God told him to. Miriam and

Aaron were following Moses' lead because God told them to. When they decided to resist Moses' leadership, they suddenly found themselves face-to-face with an angry God whose authority they had challenged. It must have been a sobering moment. God hates rebellion, and He always brings severe judgment on it. Miriam, the chief accuser, was afflicted with leprosy, the most despised and feared disease of that day.

Moses interceded for Miriam and was quick to forgive, but note that Aaron, as the high priest, was the one who had to pronounce her clean. Isn't that interesting? Miriam was judged through the leprosy and ultimately healed, but she is not mentioned again as a member of the leadership team. Her rebellion and breaking of relationship disqualified her for a leadership role. She had failed to deal with the changing face of shared ministry and was removed from the picture entirely.

Aaron would face his own difficulties in dealing with the emergence of young Joshua in the leadership team. Exodus 24:13 says, "Then Moses set out *with Joshua* his aide, and Moses *went up on the mountain of God*. He said to the elders, '*Wait here* for us until we come back to you. *Aaron* and Hur are with you....' " This is a picture of the changing face of shared ministry.

Suddenly Aaron is left behind to mind the store while young Joshua gets to climb the forbidden mount of God with Moses. Aaron used to climb that mountain with Moses, but no more. Now there's a new boy on the block. By the way, it was during this trip up the mountain that Aaron caved in to public pressure to build the golden calf. Could it be that Aaron's inability to deal with Joshua's emergence in leadership played into his failure at the foot of the mountain? It takes a lot of grace and obedience to be an Aaron. Moses was angry when he saw what Aaron had done and he said, "What did these people do to you?" (Ex. 32:21)

Meanwhile, Joshua was being carefully prepared to take the lead after Moses' death. Exodus 33:11 says, "The Lord would speak to Moses face to face, as a man speaks with his friend. Then Moses would return to the camp, *but his young aide Joshua, son of Nun did not leave the tent* [of Presence]." Joshua was learning what it was to linger in the Presence of God, because God was going to bring him through into ministry.

None of God's choices for the original leadership team were wrong. Each person had something vital to contribute, yet the team began to disintegrate because they failed to effectively deal with the pressures of shared ministry. The four leaders in the Book of Exodus were yoked together to bring about God's purposes as a team, but the pressures separated the team before its time. We need to learn how to "stay together" as a team.

How to Stay Together In Team Ministry

1. *Have realistic expectations.* Don't naively expect to live together forever in total harmony. Have realistic expectations. The leadership team needs to be hard to get into but easy to get out of. We usually do things

the other way around by making it easy to get in but hard to get out of leadership circles. Yes, we should take relationships and responsibilities seriously, but we should also *release one another very easily* so people won't feel they're under obligation. Leadership relations should be free and voluntary.

2. *Learn how to communicate in a two-way forum.* Have you ever been in team situation where people won't talk? It encourages people to make wrong assumptions. There needs to be strong communication in leadership teams. It's kind of like in marriage—communication is the bottom line. Talk with one another and spend time together.

3. *Strive for honesty and openness.* I like nice meetings as much as anybody else, and I don't like aggravation. But I would rather see people talk bluntly in total honesty then conceal the truth or an area of irritation just to avoid offending me. We've got to be open, honest, and even willing to *confront* when necessary.

4. *Give time to friendship as well as time to business.* Very often, ministry teams will find themselves totally wrapped up in situations, or in mundane things like official minutes and discussions, that they don't actually get to know one another. True ministry teams are joined at the heart as friends and covenant partners, not just linked at the head or by shared titles.

5. *Pray together.* The ministry team that prays together rarely ends up in deadlocks over issues.

6. *Avoid cynicism and barbed comments.* I've been in team meetings where I was surprised at the small negative barbs flying around the room in the discussions. We

have had to say to one another, "Let's leave behind the sarcasm and little comments about one another. Let's walk in the light together, and avoid cynicism and barbed comments."

7. *Learn the importance of support and affirmation.* We have already talked about this point, but it is extremely important to the health of any ministry team.

8. *Recognize the changing face of shared ministry* Recognize that things change. Don't cling to some nostalgic view of church "when everything used to be wonderful." It really wasn't that great, you know. Things change. God is bringing new people into the leadership mix to meet the challenges of growth tomorrow. *Don't get nostalgic; get prophetic.*

The Ministry Team of Ascension Gifts

The apostle Paul made it crystal clear in Ephesians 4 that God has ordained that ministry gifts be released into the Church of Jesus Christ.

It was He [Jesus Christ] *who gave some to be apostles, some to be prophets, some to be evangelists, and some to be pastors and teachers, to prepare God's people for works of service, so that the body of Christ may be built up until we all reach unity in the faith and in the knowledge of the Son of God and become mature, attaining to the whole measure of the fullness of Christ* (Ephesians 4:11-13).

God ordained what we call "the ascension gifts" so that unity of the faith would burst into the Christian scene. Jesus Christ released all five ministry gifts to help equip each individual member of the Church for the *work of the ministry* so we can reach *unity in the faith.* God's hand is literally "the hand of anointed leadership." We need to be praying that God will raise up apostles, prophets, evangelists, pastors, and teachers *so that the grasp of God can be felt on the Church again.*

There needs to be a re-emergence of apostolic and prophetic ministry that pushes the Church beyond where it is now. If we want to see the hand of God on the Church in revival, then we must see the hand of anointed leadership rise up. (This becomes a problem, of course, for anyone who doesn't accept human leadership.)

I'm not just saying that every local church needs five people who are "special." We simply need to see a release of ministries across the Church so that the grasp of God can be upon our cities and nations. You may already be familiar with the metaphoric comparison of the "fivefold ministry" of Ephesians 4 and the human hand, but I want to conclude this chapter with this simple illustration of purpose and interaction among these gifts.

Look at your extended hand, beginning with your little finger. The little finger represents the teacher. It is virtually impossible to move your little finger without causing every other part of your hand to move as well. The teacher is like this little finger; it influences the rest. A teaching ministry in the Church will influence all the other ministries. It provides a foundation in God's Word that affects every other part. That explains why teachers face a stricter judgment before God.

The second finger, the ring finger, symbolizes the pastor. This covenant member speaks of relationship. Pastors let us feel the grasp of God in the area of shepherding. They impart the love and nurturing of the Father heart of God that beats throughout the Church.

The middle finger is slightly bigger and sometimes extends further out than the rest. This speaks symbolically of the evangelist, who is meant to be out beyond the sheepfold, pioneering and gathering converts outside the Shepherd's fold.

The prophet, of course, gets the classic "pointing finger." The prophet "tells you" what is on the heart of God and points the way.

Finally, the thumb represents the apostle who touches all the rest. The apostle touches all the ministries. He draws in and works with each of these ministries. At times, he may even bring opposing force to bring balance and greater grasping power to the whole. Together, these ascension gifts can bring the grasp of God to the Church as the ultimate ministry team in the Church. We need to recognize them and release them to operate together in their calling. Then the many-membered Church will enter new levels of wholeness, unity, and power as fully equipped and unified ministers of reconciliation.

Endnotes

1. *Comprehensive Standard Dictionary* (Funk & Wagnalls, 1934).

2. *Comprehensive Standard Dictionary.*

3. *Comprehensive Standard Dictionary.*

4. *Comprehensive Standard Dictionary.*

Chapter 9

Pursue God's Vision

After traveling all over Europe for three years with British Youth for Christ trying to bring young people to Jesus, I became disillusioned. My heart broke when I saw so many new believers "slip through the net" and back into the world. They failed to become rooted in local churches where they could be nurtured and brought to maturity. That helped turn my heart toward pastoral ministry, and I seemed to lose all excitement over evangelism as I'd known it. I quietly resisted "too much talk" about evangelism, missions, and growth, thinking, *We've got enough problems here without all that. Let's get our act in order first.*

When God sovereignly touched me through the renewal and revival sweeping across England and the world today, He planted a fresh burden in my heart to move out of my "maintenance mentality" into a "mission mentality." God is pushing us out of our comfortable church meetings and nice meeting facilities because His vision is to see the Church impact the world! He wants us to have a heart for cities, for entire regions, and for the nations. He wants us to pour our lives and resources into the harvest *and* to maintain and nurture what He gives us.

Will more pressure come with progress and growth? Without a doubt. Yet God is preparing us for the great harvest by showing us how to develop effective ministry teams, unshakable relationships, and deep friendships to help us bear the burden of God together in unity. This in turn will bring even more of God's blessing upon us so that we may be a greater blessing to others.

How Do We Maintain Our Vision?

At the age of eight, I had already sensed God was talking to me about revival. Later, as a teenager, I opened a booklet with a little phrase at the bottom that said, "Someone needs to light a fire in your city, will it be you?" I remember thinking, *Well, I guess it never could be, but I'll have a go.* Then I said out loud, "Lord, if there is any way that I could light a flame in the city of Lincoln, that's what I want to do." Once again, the Lord was listening.

I believe God calls us, speaks to us, and plants holy desires in our hearts. It may be difficult at times to comprehend and then express the things He has deposited in us, but it is usually even more difficult to see them come to fruition in our lives because of the pressures and obstacles we've already mentioned.

I was privileged to hear Bob Mumford share from Psalm 139 on "the all-knowing, all-seeing God" who knows everything about us. It took me back to my nineteenth year when I first encountered that strange breed of people called Pentecostals. They frightened me to death at the beginning, but I was impacted by the power and Presence of God in their meetings, and I received the baptism of the Holy Ghost at that time.

I deeply appreciate the revelation of God's power I received in those years, but in the last few years, I've begun to rediscover the intimacy of the friendship of God in fresh ways. As Bob Mumford opened the truths of God's Word, I began to understand as never before that God knows everything about me—and He chooses to love me and fellowship with me anyway!

"Oh Lord, You have searched me and You know me" (Ps. 139:1). God knows us, and He knows our aspirations as leaders. He knows the call He has placed on each of us along with the burdens we go through. One verse in particular challenged me. Psalm 139:16b says, "All the days ordained for me were written in Your book before one of them came to be."

I thought, *Could it be that there is a God who knows my actions before I act, knows my thoughts before I think them, knows my words before I speak them, knows my beginning before I was born?* I thought of the times I'd said, "Well, God, You can't use me. I'm too insignificant." Then Bob Mumford took us to Philippians 3:12, where Paul told the Philippians, "Not that I have already obtained all this, or have already been made perfect, but I press on *to take hold of* **that** for which Christ Jesus took hold of me." I immediately thought, *Lord, I want to get hold of that.*

1. **By Finding "That."** Perhaps the biggest problem we face in our search is that there just isn't much explanation about what "that" is! Most of us feel a sense of destiny about God's call on our lives, and we desperately want to take hold of "that." We just can't seem to grasp what "that" is, exactly. I was grappling with this verse in Philippians when the revelation began to come in the form of a question. Saul was walking down a road when the sky lit up and the ascended Jesus apprehended him and called him to his destiny. Now Jesus had a definite plan and purpose for Saul,

but I began to almost hear Saul cry out in these verses:

*Lord, what was it that You had in Your mind for me the day You apprehended me? What did You arrest me for? Because I want **that**!*

God wants you and I to each find our "that." Your "that" isn't my "that." And my "that" isn't your "that." It also seems that this mysterious "that" we are seeking isn't always bound up exclusively in some Christian ministry, a leadership platform, or a position in the Church. It is really found in the answer to one great question above all others: "Lord, what did You have in Your mind for me the day You apprehended me and took hold of me? What do You have in Your heart for me?"

The only way you and I can maintain vision in the midst of all the pressures we face is by finding our "that." You can't always define it or frame "that" in a simple sentence, but I'm beginning to find a bit of clarity for it in my own life. I've often battled with pressure to do things I wasn't really equipped or anointed to do. I felt pressured to evangelize or to preach in particular ways I wasn't gifted to do, but now I hear God saying to me, "I want you to come into *that* to which I've called you." In the words of C.S. Lewis, God is calling me to "nothing more and nothing less" than His "that" for me, not the desires, programs, and agendas others would impose on me.

In my case, God has called me simply to serve the Church. I can't tell you all the ramifications of serving the Church, but I know that this is my "that." The Church is where I want to be, and I feel God is bringing me into my pages of destiny. God also wants to bring you into His "that" for your life.

2. **By Formulating "That."** Contrary to our first impressions, we are not talking about something that is "out there" in the untouchable, incomprehensible realm of ether or existentialism. God not only calls us individually to fulfill a specific destiny in Him, but He also puts us into specific local congregations to complete a special "mix" of gifts and abilities. Paul told the Corinthian congregation, "But now hath God set the members every one of them in the body, as it hath pleased Him" (1 Cor. 12:18 KJV). Why? It's so we can apprehend a specific "that" unique to each local gathering. God is calling us as corporate expressions of His Body to *formulate "that"* with His assistance and guidance.

First of all, we began to see a wonderful move of the Holy Spirit in our gatherings that brought fresh life, color, and release to our members.

Secondly we noticed that God was especially blessing our focus on the "Alpha Courses," a foundational discipleship program developed in England. I don't jump up and down over programs of any type generally, but God specifically directed us to use the Alpha Courses to properly ground and disciple new believers in our fellowship. It went far to calm my old haunting fears about new babes in Christ falling away through inattention, poor discipleship, and lack of basic training in God's Word.

Thirdly, I was surprised to see that God was especially blessing our attempts to bring organization to our structure and activities as a local family of Christ. It was only through the Lord's wonderful outpouring of the Holy Spirit that we were able to set into place structure and organization in ways that we really hadn't seen before. His manifest Presence among us brought healing and unity on a level we'd never experienced, and more and more people have been motivated to work in anointed teams with more accountability and responsibility.

This formulation process actually began the day a businessman from our church body came to me and said, "What is the vision of the church?" I said, "You've been here a long time. I thought you would know." He shook his head and said, "No, I'm not asking whether *I know* what the vision is. I want to know if *you* know what the vision of the church is?"

After muttering a long, "W-e-l-l..." I stepped into the "spiritual waffle mode." It sounded much like *your* spiritual waffle mode: "Well, *of course* I know what the vision is...I mean, you've been here long enough to know what the vision of this church is, and of course I know the vision."

Unimpressed, the man said, "Well, what is it then?" So I said, "It's a very simple, straightforward vision." Again he said, "Well, what is it?" At this point, I began to seriously seek a genuine answer, and I pulled all the other leaders and many others into the process—beginning with my businessman friend. "Look, I think I know what it is, but I think I could do with some help."

With the help of this man and one or two others, we went through every department and area of the church and we began to ask awkward questions (the businessman didn't need any practice, but I did). We began to say, "Perhaps we don't have the clarity that we need," and we began to formulate "that."

As we asked ourselves, "What is it that God is calling us to?" we settled on the fact that He was calling us in particular to become a large, strategic, city center church. This was confirmed through numerous prophecies, including one given through Dale Gentry. This man was almost irritating because he seemed to know more about our corporate "that" than we did! He prophesied by the Spirit that there was going to be a great move of the Holy Spirit in this city in the university. The only problem was (and the skeptics among us were quick to point it out) that *there wasn't a university in the city of Lincoln!*

You can imagine our shock when two weeks later, everyone in Lincoln received literature advertising the fact that "the new University of Lincoln" was going to be built within a stone's throw of our building! Only two weeks before, this visiting minister had said that our move back to the building God had given us was more strategic than we realized! At this writing, students have already begun to arrive to attend classes within a stone's throw of our building. Before the end of the century, more than 5,000 college students will be living and studying next to us—we're the nearest church. God knew that and He sent a prophet to proclaim and confirm His plans.

Fourthly, God is blessing our determination and focused efforts to "strain" and press forward in His calling for us. Paul uses the athletic terms *straining* and *pressing* to describe his efforts in ministry (see Phil. 3:12-14).

This suggests that it will not always be easy, and that there will be obstacles to overcome. The problem with this kind of message is our tendency to think, *Well I'm not a Paul, and my destiny and my book will be pretty thin.* I tell you that God has a purpose and a plan for you and for your church fellowship. You are more important than you think. You are more special in God's sight than you could ever imagine.

You need to press through and take hold of "that." Your nation needs leaders who are determined to press through, to strain forward into God and declare, "Lord, with all my heart and with all my inadequacies, I want to take hold of *that* for which You have taken hold of me!" As we seek our "that" individually and corporately, God's purposes will begin to be revealed in our cities, regional areas, and entire nations!

Paul wrote, "Brothers, I do not consider myself yet to have taken hold of it. But one thing I do: *Forgetting what is behind and straining toward what is ahead*" (Phil. 3:13). Paul spoke of forgetting the past and of straining toward what is *ahead*. God is doing a new thing in the earth today, but many segments of the Church seem to clinging to the past and pining over "what used to be." We need to learn some invaluable lessons from Paul and from Saul, David, and Solomon.

I believe one of the most important questions church leaders can ask today is this: "Who is going to pick up the baton and run the race?" If this present move of God is to genuinely impact the world, then the generations must work together as never before! I believe that God is pleased when people speak of "the God of Abraham, Isaac, and Jacob." He wants the generations to move together into His promises and blessings.

Sadly, Church history is not on our side. People often get bored with existing structures and decide they want to begin new things—quite apart from God's direction. Our prayer should be that the God of Abraham, Isaac, and Jacob will allow us to push forward into the future in unity, so there will be a continuation of the work of God for many decades and generations. Frankly, a lot of this depends on how we approach the future and the changes it requires. We need to understand the purposes of God for the next millennium and make plans for a smooth transition into those purposes.

> **God is looking for a strong Church that has learned the lessons of the past and is ready to move *forward* into all that He has planned for it.**

God is working out His purposes in us, and we need to relax into that. Yet there is a sense of urgency, of the need for us to strain toward what is ahead in God. That means that change is inevitable, and every generation has found that change is more difficult than we'd like to admit.

Preparing for the Future

The Bible contains some vital principles for preparing for the future, and they focus on *attitudes*. These attitudes are illustrated in the reign of three kings: Saul, David, and Solomon. They directly affected how governing authority and ministry were transferred from Saul to David, and then from David to Solomon. Each of these men reigned for 40 years, but the fruits of their reigns were radically different.

There are two basic ways to approach change and the future. The first approach is illustrated in the life of Saul in First Samuel 18. Remember that we are looking at principles and not individuals. So when we think of Saul, we're thinking of how the people in one era were preparing for the next era in terms of leadership and life.

Three Symptoms of a Failed Future

1. *Mixed messages.* When King Saul first brought young David into his household, the young man sometimes felt he was wanted, and then he felt totally rejected. Sometimes he felt like he was the man for the future, and at other times he felt rejected and hurt, as a victim of Saul's jealousy. Saul sent David very mixed messages.

   Positive: "From that day Saul kept David with him and did not let him return to his father's house" (1 Sam. 18:2). At first, Saul's actions seemed to tell David, "I want you in my household. I don't want you to go home."

   Negative: "The next day an evil spirit from God came forcefully upon Saul. He was prophesying in his house, while David was playing the harp, as he usually did. Saul had a spear in his hand and he hurled it, saying to himself, 'I'll pin David to the wall.' But David eluded him twice" (1 Sam. 18:10-11). Mixed messages.

   Positive/Negative: "Saul said to David, 'Here is my older daughter Merab. I will give her to you in marriage; only serve me bravely and fight the battles of the Lord' " (1 Sam. 18:17a). After trying to pin David to the wall with a spear, Saul tells David that he wants him to marry his daughter! Saul secretly hoped the Philistines would kill David, and when David successfully battles the Philistines, Saul again tried to spear David while he was playing his harp. This time David escaped from the palace (see 1 Sam. 19:9-10).

This generation faces a real danger of sending mixed messages to the next generation as we strain toward the future. The key lies in our attitudes and heart motives.

2. *Jealousy and lack of support.* Look at what happened when some of David's supporters began to sing a little ditty about their favorite young warrior:

> *As they danced, they sang: "Saul has slain his thousands, and David his tens of thousands." Saul was very angry; this refrain galled him. "They have credited David with tens of thousands," he thought, "but me with only thousands. What more can he get but the kingdom?" And from that time on Saul kept a jealous eye on David* (1 Samuel 18:7-9).

Saul knew that David was actually better at certain things than he was. Now if Saul had possessed a different disposition, perhaps he would have been thankful to God that he was a "thousands man." The fact that God had given him a loyal and submissive "tens of thousands man" who could lead the people of God into the next generation should have filled his life with joy, but he was jealous.

We see the same scenario time and again in changing church situations. Yes, we want the new to come through, but we secretly hope the new folks won't do a better job than we could do. Why? It's a bit of a threat to us. (This applies to virtually every person and function in church life.) We have to be very careful about the issue of jealousy, and we need to support others—even those who are better than we are at various tasks and functions.

3. *There was no planning for the future.* Saul seemed to be always living solely for the day at hand. He only seemed to be interested in his own reputation and the here and now. That helps explain why he was not prepared for David to come onto the scene.

151

These three areas represent very real stumbling blocks that we need to avoid as we strain forward into the future God has for us. Obviously, Saul didn't do a particularly good job in preparing for David. The Bible presents a very different picture of David's reign and the way he prepared for the transition of authority and ministry to Solomon. Perhaps one reason David is known as such a great king is because *he had an eye for the future.* Very often in his prayers, David asked the Lord to be faithful "to the house of David for eternity." He was looking to the future and straining toward what was ahead.

The transition to Solomon (his very name means "peace, peaceful, or safety") presents a picture of the people of God coming into a time of peace. After the struggles, after the battles, after the ground has been won by one generation, the next generation can come along and enjoy the fruits without the warfare, the heartache, or the bloodshed. The next generation of the Church should be able to spread the glory even more effectively because of our diligent labor in this era.

I believe that the next generation should not have to go through all the hassles, problems, and pains we had to go through. You shouldn't have to start all over again and reinvent the wheel. No, the victories we win today should become the foundation for totally new conquests by the next generation. There should be progress into new areas of God's plan, not merely maintenance of what we have today or had yesterday.

The believers who were sent before my generation fought difficult battles and were often ostracized for their faith and hunger for "more." I thank God for the early Pentecostals who were unable sometimes to hold down jobs because of the persecution that came upon them at the beginning of the century. They were even ostracized by the organized church.

We don't have to fight that battle again. Thanks to their sacrifices, we can go on to new frontiers for Christ. They passed the baton to us, now we need to pass it on to the next generation. King David set a pattern of principles for us to follow if we want to successfully receive God's vision and prepare for the future.

Three Symptoms of a Successful Future

1. *Shared vision.* How would you feel if you got a vision and someone else fulfilled it? Very often, I've come up with an ingenious idea in my sleep that I just knew would be successful. Then I would see that invention show up in a store or in an advertisement with someone else's name on it, and I'd think, *Hey, I thought of that first. That was my idea!*

   David must have felt that way about his idea to build God a "house" or temple. God told him, "You are not the one to build Me a house to dwell in" (1 Chron. 17:4b). Nathan the prophet also told David:

   ...I declare to you that the Lord will build a house for you: when your days are over and you go to be with your fathers, I will raise up your offspring to succeed you, one of your own sons, and I will establish his kingdom. He is the one who will build a house for Me, and I will establish his throne forever. I will be his father, and he will be My son. I will never take My love away from him, as I took it away from your predecessor. I will set him over My house and My kingdom forever; his throne will be established forever (1 Chronicles 17:10-14).

   It's not the easiest thing in the world to say, "Well, okay, Lord" to an announcement like this. But instead of sulking, David started to share his dream and his building plans with Solomon.

I constantly urge young believers to walk alongside older Christians. I tell them, "God has given us some plans. We've already laid a foundation. We've already paid the price and laid some building plans, but there are some pieces missing. We may not see the fulfillment of everything we're longing for, but it will happen—and it will probably happen *through you*." I tell older believers and leaders, "We've got to invest in the future so we'll be ready for the next wave of God's glory."

2. *Challenge and blessing.* David "charged" or challenged Solomon with the responsibility to fulfill a heavenly vision. This is thoroughly biblical. Moses charged Joshua, Paul charged Timothy, Jesus charged the disciples, and God is charging us! The generation that will bless, charge, and commit the work of God to the next generation will see a growing Church explode into the twenty-first century. As David came to the end of his life, he told Solomon:

"I am about to go the way of all the earth," he said. *"So be strong, show yourself a man, and observe what the Lord your God requires: Walk in His ways, and keep His decrees and commands, His laws and requirements, as written in the Law of Moses, so that you may prosper in all you do and wherever you go, and that the Lord may keep His promise to me..."* (1 Kings 2:2-4).

Just as God's promise to David was wrapped up in the future of Solomon, so are God's promises to the Church wrapped up in those who will follow us in the faith. We need to be a people who will charge the next generation to press through and take hold of God's promises.

David delivered a great challenge to Solomon, although David's son would end in weakness what he began in strength. We don't know what the future will hold, but history tells us that if things are left alone to follow their own desires and devices with no vision or accountability, then the fire in a fellowship will tend to grow dim. A generation that pushes through may begin in the Spirit and yet end in the flesh. Our prayer should be for a people and new generation who will grasp hold of the baton and strain forward to firmly grasp all the promises of God for their generation. The transition must be marked by challenge and blessing.

3. *Recognition and authority.* When the time came for David to begin to make room for Solomon as the next king, David wasn't content to merely "make room." He became personally and actively involved in the transition of power. He personally arranged to publicly *recognize* Solomon as the king designate and to publicly confer his *authority* on him as the new king of Israel.

[King David] *said to them: "Take your lord's servants with you and set Solomon my son **on my own mule** and take him down to Gihon. There have Zadok the priest and Nathan the prophet **anoint him king** over Israel. Blow the trumpet and **shout, 'Long live King Solomon!'** Then you are to go up with him, and **he is to come and sit on my throne** and **reign in my place.** I have appointed him ruler over Israel and Judah"* (1 Kings 1:33-35).

King David left no room for speculation or doubt, which was wise given the fact that others coveted the throne. First David ordered his leading men in the realm of civil government, military power, and spiritual authority, to publicly place Solomon on the "king's mule." No one was to ride the king's mule but the king or someone he wished to honor in a significant way (recall how King Xerxes honored Mordecai the Jew in Esther 6:7-8). David wasn't sending mixed messages—he was going to great lengths to remove any possibility of doubt or misunderstanding about his intentions. Unlike David, many church leaders have become "corks in the bottle" doing everything they can to keep the new wine from emerging.

David went even farther and ordered his son to literally sit on his throne even before he had passed away! There are no mixed signals here! Look closely at the heart motive revealed in First Kings 1:48: "...Praise be to the Lord, the God of Israel, who has allowed my eyes to see a successor on my throne today." Are you ready to praise God for losing your job, for His placing someone else on your throne? This is the very stuff of the Christian life! We need to thank God that He's bringing others into the mix, and we need to freely give them recognition and authority.

Three Keys for the Coming Generation

Saul didn't get it right, but David did. Perhaps one of the reasons David did so well in preparing for Solomon was because he remembered his days as a "king-in-waiting" and so laid a proper foundation of attitude and action. Look closely at three things David did to properly position himself for

God's blessing as the leader of the next generation after King Saul.

1. *He would not touch the Lord's anointed.* David was clearly better at certain things than King Saul. He was better in battle and wiser in strategy, and he was closer to God than Saul ever was. Yet David would not touch the Lord's anointed nor *grasp authority for himself.* In First Samuel 24:6, David told his men, "...The Lord forbid that I should do such a thing to my master, the Lord's anointed, or lift my hand against him, for he is the anointed of the Lord." The only valid authority is the authority that is *given* to you.

2. *He remained submissive and teachable.* Have you noticed that David didn't really emerge in his full potential until *after* Saul's death? That is a very sad statement. Saul should have handed things off before he died, but he didn't. He died without ever dealing with the future. David, for his part, refused to grasp at the title God had promised him in prophecy. He refused to avenge himself for terrible wrongs done against him. He refused to parlay his enormous public popularity into political favor and strength. He remained submissive and teachable.

There is no room in God's Kingdom for arrogance and pride. God has dealt quite strongly with my attitude toward various church denominations and leaders. We *must* remain submissive and teachable to those who have gone before us, without being arrogant or proud. Change will surely come, and at times we'll have to stand against things that are really not right, but let's remain submissive and teachable.

3. *He walked in humility and obedience to God.* David gave his life to God and was content and determined to become king in God's time, in God's way. As a result, he became the greatest king Israel had ever known.

God has given us the plans for His temple. He has shown us the things that are truly important in church life. To the new generation I say, "Don't be a generation that does what my generation did, which is to split off and start all over again. It is vitally important that we stand together in the things of God and bring a smooth transition from generation to generation to the glory of God and the expansion of His Kingdom."

A Word to the "Anchor Generation"

I have to give another exhortation to the members of my generation in the Church: Don't expect things to look, feel, and sound the way they always have. We've already noted how Church government and structure in the first century was dramatically different from those of today. In fact, most of what we would call "churches" today were really "house churches" or what we call cell groups today. The only entity called a "church" in Paul's day was the whole body of believers in a city or region. That's why Paul addressed his letters to "the church at Ephesus" instead of "The Second Church of St. Paul in West Ephesus."

I'm bringing this up because the "Church" as we know it is already taking radically new and different forms to meet the changing needs of the new generation. One of the phenomenon rising up in the British Church as a result of the renewal is the growth of "new churches." Some of these churches are made up entirely of young people—with young people leading them. Many of these "new churches" have a mission to reach the youth of the city, and since England's youth have been virtually cut off from the Church for two or more generations, they must be reached by very unconventional means. These churches tend to have a "dance culture" approach and relate to the nightclub scene that dominates the life of youth in England. Most of the "new churches" are related to more "conventional churches" and remain open to the advice and counsel of more mature Christian leaders. This strong and unconventional move of God shouldn't be surprising to serious students of revival. Most of the revivals in Church history started among people who caught the fire of God.

Other believers have been led to start "secular for-profit businesses" as tools of outreach to the unsaved in totally unchurched populations. By virtually every biblical standard concerning motives, functions, gifts, and vision, these "businesses" seem to qualify for the title of "church" as much as many traditional churches do.

Whatever else may come along, one thing is for certain: This worldwide move of God is calling on us to make some changes in our thinking about what a "church" really is and what it isn't. As the "anchor generation," we can function as the anchor runner in a race and by our efforts become a platform for progress into the twenty-first century, or we can become a "boat anchor" of hindrance denying the next generation freedom to catch the winds of God. The most important thing is that Jesus Christ be obeyed, honored, and glorified in all things as we pursue God's vision.

Chapter 10

Become a Church of Influence

You are the light of the world. A city on a hill cannot be hidden. ... In the same way, let your light shine before men, that they may see your good deeds and praise your Father in heaven (Matthew 5:14,16).

God doesn't seem to be interested in our keeping our faith a secret, and I think it's accurate to say He hasn't been particularly pleased with the impact the Church has had on the world over the last 20 years or so. In the eyes of the unsaved world, the Church has carried the image of weakness, apathy, hypocrisy, division, pettiness, self-centeredness, and even corruption at times. We've seemed more in love with ourselves, our money, and our personal pursuits than we have with Jesus and His passion for the lost. Thank God for renewal and revival!

The fresh breath of God on the Church has fanned the smoldering fires of righteousness, power, wisdom, and bold witness for Christ in our hearts. Things are changing and that change is happening quickly. God has stepped on stage and

He is out to change us and rearrange us until we become a *Church of influence.* As usual, when God does His part, He also expects us to do our part. "Our part" is the subject of this final chapter.

The Church that walks into the next millennium must walk in God's wisdom and skillfully use the five keys of power provided by the Lord. I am convinced that the *real key to revival* is the appearance of miraculous signs and wonders in the Church and in believers' lives. These open demonstrations of God's supernatural power can instantly cut through centuries of muddy human thought and generations of heathenism. But God can only entrust this kind of power to a wise and knowledgeable Church that carries His Son's name in honor and integrity.

The Church That Walks in Wisdom

As we move toward the close of one millennium and the birth of another, we will hear all kinds of things being said in or about the Church of Jesus Christ. A river of rumors about "the Antichrist" and of all kinds of odd disturbing comments will come like a flood, insinuating that the Lord will return at any second. Although this is possible, it is my belief that the Bible says no man (and the Greek means "no man") will know about it if He is planning to return soon. He may come soon, but most of the people alive in the world have yet to hear the precious name of the Lord spoken, let alone hear the full gospel of Jesus Christ preached to them.

The unpredictable and unstable environment that this river of rumor will create may signal the death knell of any local or denominational church structure that isn't firmly anchored in God's wisdom. They will be blown here and there by every wind of change or new doctrine of man. What is wisdom? My old *Comprehensive Standard Dictionary* says *wisdom* is "the power of true and just discernment" and "the ability to choose that which is right, sound judgment."

The only way for the Church to exercise sound judgment and discern what is right is to reject the agenda of the world in favor of the agenda revealed in the Word of God. I recently read that seven out of ten Christian teens in the United States felt it was acceptable to sleep with someone before marriage! Where did these young people come up with these ideas? It surely wasn't the Word of God.

Wisdom is prominent throughout the Bible. Wisdom and wise discernment are apparent throughout the life and ministry of Jesus, the disciples of the Lamb, and the apostle Paul. They should also be apparent in every aspect of our lives and ministry.

The Sources of Wisdom

1. *God is the source of all wisdom.* If we want to be wise, we must walk with God. Proverbs 13:20a says, "He who walks with the wise grows wise." We want to walk in wisdom, and the source of all wisdom is the Lord. A full eight chapters at the beginning of the Book of Proverbs are devoted to wisdom. In fact, wisdom is personified as a "person" in verse after verse. The sum of it all actually appears right at the beginning in Proverbs 1:7, which says, *"The fear of the Lord is the beginning of knowledge,* but fools despise wisdom and discipline." Proverbs 9:10 completes the equation with this statement: "The fear of the Lord is the beginning of wisdom, and knowledge of the Holy One is understanding." We need to fear the Lord. That's the starting point. As we demonstrate awe and respect for God, and as we reverence Him, we start on the road

to being wise and living wisely. There are no short cuts for this. Our behavior patterns will be determined by the time we spend with the Lord.

2. *A second source of wisdom is good parenting.* The first few chapters of Proverbs 1 begin with the same basic phrase: "Listen, my son, to *your father's instruction* and do not forsake *your mother's teaching*" (Prov. 1:8). Again and again, verses in these chapters begin with "my son, my son." Solomon is saying, "If you want wisdom, wise counsel, and understanding, then listen to your parents." This factor seems to be conspicuously missing from modern society and even from the Church, doesn't it?

Christian parents need to pay attention to God's priorities. He never intended for us to delegate our parenting responsibilities to prime time television stars, the news media, an endless string of baby-sitters, or some godless TV producer who is out to make a lot of money quickly at the expense of our children. We have to *make time* to share with our children the things God has shown us.

Wisdom Is a Prerequisite for the Church of Influence

Listen to what God says through Solomon as counsel to us as individuals and as members of His Church:

Get wisdom, get understanding; do not forget my words or swerve from them. Do not forsake wisdom, and she will protect you; love her, and she will watch over you. Wisdom is supreme; therefore get wisdom. Though it cost all you have, get understanding. Esteem her, and she will exalt you; embrace her, and she will honor you. She will set a garland *of grace on your head and **present you with a crown of splendor"** (Proverbs 4:5-9).*

God wants to present His Church with a crown of splendor, but first she must "get wisdom." Now that we've pinpointed the primary sources of true wisdom, how can we grow in wisdom individually and corporately?

The Growth of Wisdom

Nearly everyone acknowledges his or her need for more wisdom. The problem comes in the vacuum we encounter somewhere between good intentions and actually living out the wisdom of God. Incredible pressures are pushing and prodding us to go against the fundamental truths and principles of God's Word—and this pressure even comes from voices within religious circles who reassure us, "Oh, you don't have to really go by what the Bible says in this modern era. Just kind of make it up as you go along."

God wants us to *grow* in wisdom just as Jesus "grew in wisdom and stature, and in favor with God and men" (Lk. 2:52). Favor, or influence, only comes after we have obtained wisdom and achieved stature by walking out our faith in obedience before God and man. God wants His Church to be a wise Church, a Church of ever-growing stature, favor, and influence in the earth.

How do we grow in wisdom? The Book of Proverbs provides the first key to growth in wisdom: "The fear of the Lord is the beginning of knowledge, but fools despise wisdom and discipline" (Prov. 1:7). The key word is *discipline.* Proverbs 3:11-12 reinforces the point: "My son, do not despise the Lord's *discipline* and do not resent His *rebuke,* because the Lord *disciplines* those He loves, as a father the son he delights in." I could never understand my mum saying to me, "This is going to hurt me a lot more than it will hurt you." When I was

165

older, I realized that my mother's discipline was a loving gesture meant to help me make a change for good in my life. God our Father disciplines those whom He loves, and a disciplined Church will be a wise Church.

Secondly, we grow in wisdom through *good behavior*. You grow in wisdom by living it out, by "practicing good" instead of "practicing bad." Good intentions are not enough. We will be judged by the things we actually do, not by the intentions we have. Believers, and the Church as a whole, will grow in wisdom as right choices are made and good behavior is practiced on a regular basis. Obedience always bears visible fruit.

The two possible destinies of the Church in the twenty-first century are accurately portrayed in two chapters of the Book of Proverbs. The Church of disobedience and folly is pictured in Proverbs 6. I have selected four of the seven condemned behaviors that will doom any man or church body to a place of disgrace and ineffectiveness in the world. In fact, the Bible says God *hates and detests* these characteristics.

1. *The Church of folly* is marked by:

    a. *Scheming hearts.* God hates "a heart that devises wicked schemes" (Prov. 6:18a). Watch out for a scheming heart, and never get involved in schemes to plan evil against sinners or saints. This was the way of Saul, satan, and Judas Iscariot.

    b. *Lying tongues.* God hates "a lying tongue" (see Prov. 6:17). This one hardly needs explanation.

    c. *Shifty eyes.* God hates "haughty eyes" (see Prov. 6:17). I call "haughty eyes" shifty eyes. There is a sense of excessive pride involved here. These eyes dart back and forth, as if hiding something. When backed into a corner, they'll blaze up and declare that they don't need God or man. Whatever you do, don't count on promises given by someone with shifty eyes.

    d. *Rushing feet.* God hates people whose feet are quick to rush into evil (see Prov. 6:18). Watch out for people who jump into things without forethought, who say, "We're doing it just because we want to do it. If you say we can't, we'll beat you there just to show you we can!"

In stark contrast to the Church of folly, Proverbs 4 pictures a wise son (and a wise Church) practicing behavior that is pleasing to God. This kind of behavior is sure to reap a harvest of blessing, favor, power, and prominence in the world.

  2. *The Church of wisdom* is marked by:

    a. *Guarded hearts.* "Above all else, guard your heart, for it is the wellspring of life" (Prov. 4:23).

    b. *Guarded tongues.* "Put away perversity from your mouth; keep corrupt talk from your lips" (Prov. 4:24). The tongue can cut people down and destroy them, or it can bless. We need to watch our tongues.

    c. *Fixed eyes.* "Let your eyes look straight ahead, fix your gaze directly before you" (Prov. 4:25). Those who walk wisely will have direction and purpose; they'll know where they're going. As Christians, we want to please the Lord and follow Him, so we must keep our eyes "fixed" on Him, looking neither to the right or to the left.

    d. *Feet carefully minded and directed.* "Make level paths for your feet and take only ways that are firm" (Prov. 4:26). Don't stand on the shifting sand of man's opinions and reasoning. Take your stand on Jesus our Rock and you will be able to withstand even the worst storms of devils and men.

The best summary I can think of concerning the Church's need for wisdom was provided by James the apostle in his epistle to the Church:

Who is wise and understanding among you? Let him show it by his good life, by deeds done in the humility that comes from wisdom. But if you harbor bitter envy and selfish ambition in your hearts, do not boast about it or deny the truth. Such "wisdom" does not come down from heaven but is earthly, unspiritual, of the devil. For where you have envy and selfish ambition, there you find disorder and every evil practice. But the wisdom that comes from heaven is first of all pure; then peace-loving, considerate, submissive, full of mercy and good fruit, impartial and sincere. Peacemakers who sow in peace raise a harvest of righteousness (James 3:13-18).

The Church of wisdom is known by her fruits. No matter how much we protest or complain, the fact is that our actions speak louder than our words. If we begin to live and act wisely, individually and as a Church united, then God will elevate us to a position of prominence and influence in the world!

Five Points of Power for the Influential Church

Ask yourself the question, "What kind of Church do we need to be to move into the next century?" One thing all of us would agree on is that we need to be a Church of *power* in the midst of disbelief and darkness. The world is looking for a Church that doesn't just talk about God. The lost are desperately looking for evidence that God really is at work in all of His power and glory today.

God wants us to align ourselves with His Word and will so we can break out of our tired stereotype of wishy-washy, powerless, lukewarm Christianity. We don't want to be wishy-washy or mediocre. We want to be people who know and exhibit the power of God in our lives. We want God's glory and power to impact our world through us as very ordinary people who have been made living trophies and walking testimonies of God's transforming power.

There are five "power points" in the Book of Hebrews that we need to tap as individual believers and as the Body of Christ. Each of these "power receptacles" have been provided to us by God *to be used* in the service of lifting up the name of His Son, Jesus Christ. If we fail to see these things in our lives and ministry, then it is our fault. God has done everything necessary to make these sources of supernatural power continually available to us.

1. *We need to know the power of the Lordship of Jesus Christ.* Most modern Christians never use the word *lordship* outside of Christian circles. The closest we can come to its original meaning today is to say that, when we say Jesus is Lord, we mean He is number one, period. If we are to be a Church that makes any waves in the future, we must begin to focus on Jesus Christ as the number one, the Lord, the greatest, by whose name everything is held together.

   In the past God spoke to our forefathers through the prophets at many times and in various ways, but in these last days He has spoken to us by His Son, whom He appointed heir of all things, and through whom He made the universe. The Son is the radiance of God's glory and the exact representation of His being, sustaining all things by His powerful word. After He had

169

provided purification for sins, He sat down at the right hand of the Majesty in heaven (Hebrews 1:1-3).

This is Jesus. He fills everything. He holds together and sustains everything by His powerful word. He is the radiance of God's glory. There is immeasurable power and authority in His Lordship. We need to be a Church that honors Jesus Christ as supreme Lord, our number one in this life and in eternity. This may sound simplistic, but the only church that will move into the next millennium and prosper will be one that honors Jesus Christ, the Son of God come in the flesh and risen from the dead. He was the perfect man and the perfect Son of God; the eternal Word sent from the Father. Keep your focus on Jesus.

God the Father has ordained that Jesus His Son shall receive the highest honor in the universe and beyond. This is the power that needs to come to us as a Church: Jesus Christ is Lord of all. He is number one; His name comes first. You can't go far wrong if every day of your life you say, "Jesus, I want to follow You. Your name is higher than any other. Jesus, You are the King." Hebrews tells us that Jesus "sat down at the right hand of God" and that His enemies are to be His footstool (see Heb. 10:12-13)! There is power in the Lordship of Jesus Christ.

2. *We need to know the power of the blood of Jesus.* "What can wash away my sin? Nothing but the blood of Jesus." No matter how clever we may get in terms of programs, strategies, and missions, unless we know the power of the purifying work of the blood of Jesus Christ, then we will never move into the next millennium as a Church of influence! It is the shed blood of

Jesus that cleanses and renews the Church. Nothing less will do, and there is nothing greater.

The first thing John the Baptist said publicly about Jesus was, "Look, the Lamb of God, who takes away the sin of the world!" (Jn. 1:29b) John was specifically linking Jesus with His role as the sacrificed Lamb, the innocent Lamb without sin or fault who would become the ultimate sin-offering of Jewish tradition and who would *forever* take away our sins. The writer of Hebrews said it bluntly: "In fact, the law requires that nearly everything be cleansed with blood, and without the shedding of blood there is no forgiveness" (Heb. 9:22).

Under the Old Covenant, God's shekinah Presence was found in the Most Holy Place where no man could come except the High Priest, and then only one time a year bearing the blood of sacrifice. Again, the Book of Hebrews tells us, "Therefore, brothers, since we have confidence to enter the most Holy Place by the blood of Jesus" (Heb. 10:19). There is a way back into the Presence of God—through the shed blood of Jesus Christ, the Son of God.

The last thing so-called civilized people want to see or talk about is blood (unless, of course, it is in a blockbuster martial arts or action film, or a primetime boxing event). That is unfortunate since *the only way their sins can be forgiven and cleansed, the only way they will ever enter God's Kingdom,* is through the *cleansing flood of Jesus' blood.* I know that some churches and preachers are compromising on this issue, but they simply don't have the authority to do so.

171

The Church without the blood is nothing more than a social club on a fast track to hell. God will hold those who compromise and discount the blood personally accountable for the souls of those they have deceived! The only path to God is a bloody path, a path leading to the cross of Jesus Christ, the innocent Son of God who personally paid the penalty for our sins and rebellion with His own lifeblood. (F.B. Meyer, one of the old commentators of the past, said this: "There is nothing in a man more precious than blood. If he gives that, he gives the best he has to give. His blood is his life, his all.")

3. *The power of the Word of God.* In any move of the Holy Spirit, there is a danger that we will become experience-centered rather than Word-centered. The Welsh Revival was a very short-lived revival, and Church historians say the evidence points to the participants' increased emphasis on the events and phenomena of the revival rather than on the Word of God being proclaimed. They rooted their faith on power and personal experience without an equally strong emphasis on God's Word to anchor their experience in the Rock of God.

Prayer is always good, but prayer guided and bolstered by the authority of God's Word and led by His Spirit is a "triple braided cord" that cannot be broken (see Eccles. 4:12). We need to have it all. We need to marry our personal encounters and experiences with God with His unchanging eternal Word. Then we will experience even more power in our ministry to others. The bottom line is this, my friend: No matter how powerful and glorious the outpouring of God's power may be, *never ever think that you don't need your Bible*. Even Jesus Christ, the Son of God, did battle in this time-proven way; "It is written...."

Many people in our television-centered age think that the Bible is boring. No, the Word of God is living and sharper than a two-edged sword! It is not "just a piece of literature." I recently heard Steve Hill, the evangelist ministering in the Brownsville revival in Pensacola, Florida, proclaim one short, simple passage from the Word of God: "...O wicked man, you will surely die..." (Ezek. 33:8), and hundreds of people ran to the front in fear for their souls under the conviction of the Holy Spirit! Never underestimate the power of the Word!

Paul said, "I'm not ashamed of the gospel of Christ" (see Rom. 1:16 KJV). Can we say the same? *The Church of Influence cannot afford to be ashamed of the gospel of Jesus Christ!* When the Word of God is proclaimed under the anointing of the Holy Spirit, it's quick and sharp. The Book of Hebrews drives home my point with unmatched power and clarity: "For the word of God is living and active. Sharper than any double-edged sword, it penetrates even to dividing soul and spirit, joints and marrow; it judges the thoughts and attitudes of the heart" (Heb. 4:12). God's Word can do things that words and negotiation can never do. It can do things in a moment; it can undo us and strike straight to the heart to bring conviction, correction, restoration, and blessing.

I've heard people complain about preachers who preached the uncompromised Word, "Why doesn't he become culturally relevant?" When the Word of

God is proclaimed, culture has very little to do with it! The God of all is the God of every culture. My Bible says that *every* knee will bow, and every tongue will proclaim that Jesus Christ is Lord—and I don't think God will need any interpreters or cultural relevancy programs to make His Word come to pass (see Phil. 2:10-11).

4. *The power of the Holy Spirit.* Any time you hear people debating over whether they should emphasize the Word or emphasize the things of the Spirit, chalk it up to foolishness and ignorance of the Word. I know I'm coming on strong here, but let God's Word put this so-called controversy into focus. According to the Bible, the Word of God is the "sword of the Spirit" (Eph. 6:17). It seems to me that only a fool would try to separate the two! The Word and the Spirit always work together. God spoke of Jesus at the River Jordan, and the Holy Spirit hovered (see Mt. 3). God spoke; the Holy Spirit worked. God speaks and the Holy Spirit hurries to perform it. Don't try to divide what God Himself refuses to separate.

Hebrews 2:4, speaking of the gospel of salvation, says, "God also testified to it by signs, wonders and various miracles, and gifts of the Holy Spirit distributed according to His will." This is a picture of the living, vital Word of God being proclaimed and then supported, verified, and demonstrated by the *power of the Spirit.* God testifies to the believer and the unsaved alike through signs, wonders, and miracles worked through the gifts and anointing of the Holy Spirit.

Don't ever think that the Holy Spirit's work is separate from the Word of God. There is power in a combination of Word and Spirit. The Word of God within us needs to be accompanied by and confirmed through signs and wonders and through outpourings of the Holy Spirit in the next millennium. The power of the Spirit is yet another signature of the Church of influence, and I am absolutely convinced it is the *secret of revival.*

Don't back off. Don't become a man pleaser. Don't become content with a shortsighted satisfaction for a comfortable congregation of nice people doing and saying nice things. Set your sights according to God's standards. Refuse to settle for anything less than Spirit-filled, power-packed, Bible-believing Christianity! The Church of influence is a Church of power—power that breaks through prejudice and judgmentalism to bring God's touch to the everyday lives of the lost and broken. We've tried the other methods and have decades of failure and wasted effort to our credit. Isn't it time to do things God's way?

5. *The power of Love.* Paul put all this into a timeless perspective in First Corinthians 13. I followed Paul's lead and placed it at the "cleanup spot" in this list of God's power points, because it is and will always remain the most powerful weapon in our arsenal of godly power. Paul described the power of love this way:

*If I speak in the tongues of men and of angels, **but have not love**, I am only a resounding gong or a clanging cymbal. If I have the gift of prophecy and can fathom all mysteries and all knowledge, and if I have a faith that can remove mountains, but have not love, I am nothing. If I give all I possess to the poor and surrender my body to the flames, but have not love, I gain nothing. … **Love never fails**…. And now these three remain:*

175

*faith, hope and love. But **the greatest of these is love*** (1 Corinthians 13:1-3,8,13).

God is love. So any power we hope to possess or demonstrate in the world must be permeated and motivated by love. The world will not be turned around merely by the power of bold evangelism and glorious outpourings of the Spirit—these things must be preceded by, accompanied by, and followed by *the power of God's love.*

I believe there is an intercessory groaning in Heaven over the Church. No, it's not because we're a particularly bad bunch; it is just that Jesus our High Priest and chief Intercessor feels the pain and sorrow of our world so dark and full of decay. God the Father is waiting for us to rise up in the fullness of Christ to spread abroad the *love of God in our hearts.* Love is the answer to the world's hurts. It is love that draws men and women to repentance. Some may come because of initial fears about eternity spent in hell, but it is the love of God that will keep them. God has given us the power of love along with all the other sources of His power so that we can be a Church of influence today, tomorrow, and in the next millennium.

If you are looking for power in your life and the life of your church, love is where it begins. First we must receive the Father's love, and then we must give it away. That's why God has had millions of believers on carpets and dirt floors around the world in this great outpouring! He's humbled us before our friends and caused us to cry hot tears of compassion for the lost. At times, some of us experienced what onlookers thought was a type of epileptic fit, but it all had to do with yielding to the Father's love.

From beginning to end, everything we have been given by God as individuals and as His Church, has been given *to be given away*. Jesus extended forgiveness and mercy that we may forgive and be merciful. He gave us hope so we in turn could encourage others. He gave us His name so we could share it with others. He made us His brothers and sisters and then sends us out to get more! Nothing we have received from God is meant to be hoarded, boxed up, or preserved in museums.

I'm not an evangelist by nature, but I am convinced that this whole move of the Spirit over the earth in this decade is to help the Church actually impact society. God wants His Church to grow. He wants to see His deposit in this generation bear a rich harvest for generations to come instead of being squandered and mishandled to the point where His deposit of anointing is lost after one generation.

That means we will have to finally move on the biblical model for "the work of the ministry." We need to release all individual believers to proclaim the gospel and carry God's power into their world as ministers of reconciliation—instead of clinging to our man-made and maintained professional hierarchy of clergy. Will there be full-time ministers? Of course, but as ministry gifts to the Church, we need to spend our time and energies raising up and equipping able ministers of the gospel in the Body of Christ. We need to see an entire spiritual nation of kings and priests arise in the glory and power of God. It is this mighty army—not just its small tithe of trainers and equippers—who will have the width, breadth, and depth of God's power needed to "fill the whole earth with His glory" (see Ps. 72:19)!

This is the picture of the Church of influence, the wise and powerful Church that will execute God's will in the earth in the great harvest. It is this purified Church that will usher in the return of the Lord Jesus Christ for His glorious Bride without spot or wrinkle. It is the Church born of Holy Spirit revival, fire, power, and love that God sees in His timeless wisdom when He speaks of the Church in His Word. We need to catch God's vision and run with it! There is a lost world waiting for God's will and purposes to be *manifested and revealed through the Church.*

D *Destiny Image*
Revival Titles

SHARE THE FIRE
by Dr. Guy Chevreau.

Do you panic when you hear the word *evangelism*? Do you feel awkward "forcing" your opinions on another? All that changes when God abundantly and freely fills you with His Spirit! In *Share the Fire* you'll learn how God has intended evangelism to be: a bold and free work of Christ in you and through you!

Paperback Book, 182p. ISBN 1-56043-688-3 Retail $8.99

THE CHURCH OF THE 3RD MILLENNIUM
by Marc A. Dupont.

Uncontrollable laughter, violent shaking, falling "under the Spirit"—can these things really be from God? Using examples from the ministries of Elijah, John the Baptist, and Jesus Himself, Marc Dupont shows that God often moves in ways that challenge traditional religious views or habits; He "offends the mind in order to reveal the heart." God's end-time Church shouldn't be satisfied with the status quo. We need to reach for more of God's Spirit—and not be surprised when He gives it to us!

Paperback Book, 182p. ISBN 1-56043-194-6 Retail $8.99

GO INSIDE THE TORONTO BLESSING—*NEW VIDEO*
by Warren Marcus.

Award-winning filmmaker Warren Marcus takes you behind the scenes where you can experience a true look at this revival with footage that has never been filmed before. You will feel like you have a front row seat at the worship services. You will witness the special prayer time when many of the miracles occur. You will see unusual "manifestations"—like those reported in prior revivals. And you will hear first-person account after account of how God has dramatically changed people's lives in this revival.

1 video (approx. 60 min.) ISBN 0-7684-0082-1 Retail $19.99

Available at your local Christian bookstore.

Internet: http://www.reapernet.com

Prices subject to change without notice.

Destiny Image
New Releases

WORSHIP: THE PATTERN OF THINGS IN HEAVEN
by Joseph L. Garlington.
Joseph Garlington, a favorite Promise Keepers' speaker and worship leader, delves into Scripture to reveal worship and praise from a Heaven's-eye view. Learn just how deep, full, and anointed God intends our worship to be.
Paperback Book, 182p. ISBN 1-56043-195-4 Retail $8.99

WHEN GOD STRIKES THE MATCH
by Dr. Harvey R. Brown, Jr.
A noted preacher, college administrator, and father of an "all-American" family—what more could a man want? But when God struck the match that set Harvey Brown ablaze, it ignited a passion for holiness and renewal in his heart that led him into a head-on encounter with the consuming fire of God.
Paperback Book, 160p. ISBN 0-7684-1000-2 (6" X 9") Retail $8.99

THE LOST ART OF INTERCESSION
by Jim W. Goll.
How can you experience God's anointing power as a result of your own prayer? Learn what the Moravians discovered during their 100-year prayer Watch. They sent up prayers; God sent down His power. Jim Goll, who ministers worldwide through a teaching and prophetic ministry, urges us to heed Jesus' warning to "watch." Through Scripture, the Moravian example, and his own prayer life, Jim Goll proves that "what goes up must come down."
Paperback Book, 182p. ISBN 1-56043-697-2 Retail $8.99

PRAY WITH FIRE
by Dr. Guy Chevreau.
How do we pray in the midst of revival? *Pray With Fire!* Dr. Guy Chevreau, of the Toronto Airport Christian Fellowship renewal team, created this inspirational resource for anyone walking in revival's fire. You'll read testimonies of people soaked in God's glory and delve into "fiery" prayers of Spirit-filled people of the past—especially those of the Master, Himself.
Paperback Book, 224p. ISBN 1-56043-698-0 Retail $8.99

Available at your local Christian bookstore.

Internet: http://www.reapernet.com

Prices subject to change without notice.